LEADERSHIP AND FORCE DEVELOPMENT

Air Force Doctrine Document 1-1

8 November 2011

BY ORDER OF THE   AIR FORCE DOCTRINE DOCUMENT 1-1
SECRETARY OF THE AIR FORCE   8 NOVEMBER 2011

SUMMARY OF CHANGES

This document is substantially revised and must be completely reviewed. The structure of the document has been changed to present information in a more cohesive manner, reducing the number of chapters from four to three. The discussion on the meaning of the term "Airman" has been completely revised (Chapter 1). The discussion on leadership has been expanded to include a historical review of leadership doctrine for the Air Force (Chapter 2). Enduring competencies have been replaced by institutional competencies (Chapter 3 and Appendix C). A new appendix has been added: The Institutional Competency List (Appendix C). The appendix containing case studies has been renamed "leadership studies" to more accurately reflect the contents, and new studies have been added (Appendix E).

Supersedes: AFDD 1-1, 18 Feb 06
OPR: LeMay Center/DDS
Certified by: LeMay Center/CC (Maj Gen David S. Fadok)
Pages: 92
Accessibility: Available on the e-publishing website at www.e-publishing.af.mil for downloading
Releasability: There are no releasability restrictions on this publication
Approved by: NORTON A. SCHWARTZ, General, USAF
          Chief of Staff

FOREWORD

The Air Force develops leaders. Leadership is a skill that we learn, develop, and practice; it is not necessarily inherited nor ingrained in our DNA. This doctrine document presents the Air Force's best practices for creating leaders and applying leadership.

Leaders do not abruptly appear fully developed and ready to perform. A growth period must occur to allow young leaders time to mature into the responsibilities required of senior institutional leaders and commanders. The force development process provides the means to develop leadership. Our Air Force requires leaders who can take warfighting to the highest possible level of success in support of our national security objectives. Those leaders are created through a process of development involving education, training, and experience coupled with ongoing mentoring by more experienced leaders. The end result is the development of Airmen capable of excelling as leaders at all levels, anywhere, anytime.

The Air Force core values are the bedrock of leadership. *Integrity First* is the basis of trust, and trust is the vital bond that unifies leaders with their followers and commanders with their units. Trust makes leaders effective, and integrity underpins trust. *Service Before Self* is the essence of our commitment to the nation. Leaders who serve selflessly inspire support from everyone in their command and promote a spirit that binds organizations into an effective warfighting team. *Excellence in All We Do* is our commitment to the highest standards of service to our country. Leaders set the standard for excellence in their organizations.

This document is *the* Air Force statement of leadership principles. Your personal leadership is the key to our Service's success in fulfilling our mission to fly, fight, and win.

NORTON A. SCHWARTZ
General, USAF
Chief of Staff

TABLE OF CONTENTS

PREFACE

Air Force Doctrine Document (AFDD) 1-1, *Leadership and Force Development*, is the Air Force's capstone doctrinal publication on leadership and how the Service uses force development to build leaders. AFDD 1-1 is a direct descendant in a line of Air Force documents chronicling leadership for the Service dating back to its earliest days. It presents the best practices of how an Airman leads and why leadership for an Airman differs from those of other Services. The three chapters and the appendices describe what an Airman is, how Airmen lead, what force development is, and how it is put into practice.

✪ Chapter 1, *The Airman*, explains what an Airman is and how the Airman's perspective is integral to his or her thinking. It gives an overview of the total force, explaining the differences in leadership by officers, enlisted members, and Department of the Air Force civilians, along with a description of the specialized leadership needs and limitations when dealing with contractors. It provides the authoritative source for the Air Force core values, along with the supporting characteristics of valor, courage, and sacrifice that are fundamental to what an Airman is. It describes the mindset an Airman needs to conduct warfighting and how the profession of arms is key to what an Airman does. The Airman's Creed is located in this chapter to show its relationship to both the concept of what an Airman is and how this creed is vital to leadership in the Air Force.

✪ Chapter 2, *Leading Airmen*, defines leadership for the Air Force. It discusses the foundations of leadership for the Service, with a historical analysis of the origins of leadership in the Air Force. It introduces the levels of leadership used in the Air Force for force development: tactical expertise, operational competence, and strategic vision. This expands the discussion of levels of leadership from the previous edition to provide greater fidelity to the concepts, along with more descriptive terminology that is more representative of how leadership is executed. It describes institutional competencies and leadership actions, and how these leadership components are key to developing leaders.

✪ Chapter 3, *Force Development*, defines the term force development for the Air Force. It describes the force development construct and the continuum of learning with its three elements of education, training, and experience. The corporate body for ensuring there is a deliberate process employed in developing the workforce is explained. Institutional competencies and how they are used to identify desired expectations for the total workforce are clarified. The institutional competency assessment strategy illustrates how graduates are surveyed to determine how well the military education and training schools have taught them to perform the institutional competency descriptive behaviors at the prescribed proficiency levels. Common guiding principles demonstrate how education, training, and experience affect the development of Airmen.

⊙ The appendices provide supporting material for the discussion of leadership and force development. The oaths of office and enlistment provide a source of leadership for the Air Force. The code of conduct for members of the Armed Forces of the United States grounds all members of the Armed Forces with the same requirements of conduct. The institutional competency list is the definitive listing of the Air Force's institutional competencies and their subcompetencies, along with their definitions. The discussion of education and training is provided to differentiate between these concepts so they can be better understood in the context of force development. The leadership studies provide real-world examples of the three levels of leadership practiced by Airmen.

The principal audience for this AFDD is all Airmen in the US Air Force. To differentiate US Air Force Airmen from other individuals in other Services and other nations who support airpower, the term **Airman** is reserved for US Air Force personnel and **airman** is used for those from other Services and nations.

As the capstone document on leadership, its application crosses all lines of rank, component, or status. This is the defining document for leadership in the US Air Force, using force development as its means of building leaders.

CHAPTER ONE

THE AIRMAN

Today, we have more than 39,000 Airmen deployed to 260 locations across the globe, as an additional 130,000 Airmen support combatant command operations from their home stations. While our operations tempo is high, you, our Nation's Airmen, continue to set the standard for excellence. We are continuously reminded of the courage, commitment, and sacrifice you offer on a daily basis.

—**Michael B. Donley,
Secretary of the Air Force (SECAF),
Memorial Day 2010**

All Airmen, military and civilian, support and defend the Constitution of the United States and live by the Air Force core values. Airmen are the foundation of the Air Force organizations and units that enable the Department of Defense to support the National Security Strategy. The term Airman has historically been associated with uniformed members of the US Air Force (officer or enlisted; regular, Reserve, or Guard) regardless of rank, component, or specialty.[1] Today, Department of the Air Force (DAF) civilians are incorporated within the broader meaning of the term when there is a need to communicate to a larger audience within the Service, either for force development purposes or for clarity and inclusiveness by senior leaders when addressing a larger body of personnel.

Airmen recognize and value airpower in its application, which is fundamentally different and more flexible than other forms of military power and instruments of national power.[2] This inherent flexibility allows our force to be applied independently or in concert with other forms of military power. The application and integration of airpower produce effects across multiple domains and theaters. Air Force forces are employed at different speeds and closure rates and over greater distances and should be applied by those who appreciate the breadth and scope of that power across the range of

---

[1] This broader meaning does not, however, mean or imply that anyone other than uniformed members of the US Air Force are members of the armed Services in other contexts. For example, in the context of punitive Air Force instructions or the law of armed conflict regulations, care must be taken to ensure that the rights and obligations imposed under those regulations are not uniformly applied to both Service members and civilians.

[2] See AFDD 1, *Air Force Basic Doctrine, Organization, and Command,* for a discussion on the Air Force's roles, missions, and Service core functions.

military operations as unique. Due to the distinctive nature of the capabilities brought to the fight, Airmen see their Service as unique.[3]

The study of airpower and the strengths of its capabilities lead to a particular expertise and a distinctive point of view that General Henry H. "Hap" Arnold termed "airmindedness."[4] The Airman's perspective is forged from horizonless operations from, in, and through the air, space, and cyberspace domains.[5] Whereas land and maritime domains each comprise a portion of the earth's surface, air, space and cyberspace—the Air Force's operating domains—surround 100% of our world.

> The Airman's perspective may be shared by members of the other Services and other nations who apply airpower. To differentiate US Air Force Airmen from these other like-minded individuals, the term **Airman** is reserved for US Air Force personnel while **airman** is used as a general term for those from various Services and nations.

THE AIRMAN'S PERSPECTIVE

The US Air Force flies, fights, and wins in air, space, and cyberspace. The Air Force provides organized, trained, and equipped forces to support combatant commanders who are responsible for deterring attacks against the United States, its territories, possessions, and bases, and employing appropriate force should deterrence fail.[6] Air, space, and cyberspace are flexible and dynamic domains that present opportunities and vulnerabilities. These vulnerabilities, when not mitigated, may be used by America's adversaries to their advantage. The Air Force is the premier American military force capable of overcoming those vulnerabilities in defense of the United States.

Airmen are essential to the successful execution of the Air Force's responsibilities in support of the combatant commanders, therefore they should understand and actively advocate the Airman's perspective on the use of airpower to achieve national objectives. Understanding the Airman's perspective gives Airmen a distinct advantage when performing the responsibilities of the Air Force. They approach mission accomplishment in a manner unique to those educated, trained, and experienced in bringing an airmindedness to all actions they perform. Airmen bring a perspective to performing the Air Force's mission that compounds their effectiveness in a manner best suited to support the Air Force, joint, and multinational fight.

Airmen normally think of airpower and the application of force from a functional rather than geographical perspective. Airmen do not divide up the battlefield into

---

[3] Maj Gen Charles Dunlap, Jr., *Understanding Airmen: A Primer for Soldiers, Military Review,* September-October 2007, 126.
[4] Gen Henry H. ("Hap") Arnold, *Third Report of the Commanding General of the Army Air Forces to the Secretary of War,* Baltimore, Md: Schneidereith, 12 November 1945, 70.
[5] Air Force Manual 1-1 (1992), *Essay U: Airmindedness: An Example.*
[6] Unified Command Plan, paragraph 10.a.

operating areas.[7] Airmen typically approach battle in terms of creating effects to meet joint force commander objectives, rather than on the nature and location of specific targets.[8] This approach normally leads to more inclusive and comprehensive perspectives that favor holistic solutions over tactical ones.

When Air Force forces are employed in various operational environments, they offer basic characteristics that, when exploited, are fundamental to the successful conduct of war and peace. These characteristics, when molded into viable force capabilities and executed by knowledgeable Airmen, enhance the overall ability of the joint force to achieve success when called upon. Therefore, each Airman should understand and be able to articulate the full potential and application of Air Force capabilities required to support the joint force and meet the nation's security requirements.

THE TOTAL FORCE

The total force consists of the people who make up the Air Force. It is defined as "the US Air Force organizations, units, and individuals that provide the capabilities to support the Department of Defense in implementing the national security strategy. Total force includes Regular Air Force, Air National Guard of the United States, Air Force Reserve military personnel, US Air Force military retired members, US Air Force civilian personnel (including foreign national direct and indirect-hire, as well as non-appropriated fund employees), contractor staff, and host-nation support personnel."[9]

The regular Air Force is defined as the component of the Air Force that consists of persons whose continuous service on active duty in both peace and war is contemplated by law, and of retired members of the regular Air Force.[10] The Air National Guard is an organized state militia and a reserve component of the Air Force. The Air National Guard of the United States is a federal organization that is also a reserve component of the US Air Force. Air National Guard Airmen serve in both organizations, and can move between them as duty requires.[11] The Air Force Reserve is a component of the United States Air Force as prescribed by law.[12] They are represented by a mix of Traditional Reservists, Individual Mobilization Augmentees, participating Individual Ready Reservists, Air Reserve Technicians, Title 32 Excepted Civil Service Technicians (Guard Technicians), and Active Guard/Reserve, both Drill Status Guardsmen and full-time forces.

---

[7] Col Dennis M. Drew, *Joint Operations: The World Looks Different from 10,000 Feet, Airpower Journal,* Fall 1988, http://www.airpower.maxwell.af.mil/airchronicles/apj/apj88/fal88/drew.html, accessed 6 Jan 09.
[8] Air Force Doctrine Document (AFDD) 1, *Air Force Basic Doctrine, Organization, and Command*; AFDD 3-60, *Targeting.*
[9] AFI 90-1001, *Responsibilities for Total Force Integration,* 29 May 07 (IC 1, 25 Apr 08).
[10] Title 10, United States Code (U.S.C.) §8075.
[11] 10 U.S.C. §101(c)(4) and (5); Perpich v. Department of Defense, 496 U.S. 334, 110 S. Ct. 2418, 110 L.Ed.2d 312 (1990).
[12] 10 U.S.C. §10101. In addition, non-participating and inactive members who are part of the Individual Ready Reserve, the Standby Reserve, and the Retired Reserve are subject to recall as authorized by law. See 10 U.S.C. §§ 10144, 10151, and 10154.

DAF civilians are members of the total force, but are not members of the above elements of the Air Force. Regular Air Force, Guard, Reserve, and DAF civilians fall under the use of the term Airman when force development issues are discussed or general inclusiveness by senior leaders is required for clarity in communication.

Air Force contractors are also members of the total force, but their connection to the Service does not rise to the same level as that of regular Air Force, Guard, Reserve, or DAF civilians, who are required to swear an oath of allegiance. Contractors support the missions of Airmen. Managing contractors requires a different leadership approach because they are not part of the military chain of command. Contractor personnel should be managed through the terms and conditions set forth in their contract. They do not normally fall under Uniform Code of Military Justice authority. Therefore, it is imperative that Air Force leaders ensure a strong contractor management system is in place in both peacetime and during contingency operations.

Upon entering the Service, Air Force officers, enlisted members, and DAF civilians take an oath,[13] signifying their personal commitment to support and defend the Constitution of the United States and a commitment and willingness to serve their country for the duration of their Air Force careers. The oath is a solemn promise to do one's duty and meet one's responsibilities. The oath of office for officers and civilians and the oath of enlistment for enlisted personnel are in Appendix A.

Officers[14]

A military officer has responsibilities as a warfighter, a servant of the Nation, a member of the profession of arms, and a leader of character. Frequently, these roles are carried out simultaneously. While officers often shoulder our Air Force's leadership responsibilities, that leadership role must be earned through demonstrated adherence to our core values and proven followership abilities. One must be a good follower in order to be a good leader. Preparation to fulfill the role of an Air Force officer is a continual developmental process. Air Force officers are raised with an Airman's perspective and grown in the culture of the Service. This perspective is developed through education in how the Air Force operates and honed through operational experience. Leadership opportunities grow throughout this developmental process as does an officer's ability to articulate the capabilities the Air Force brings to the joint fight.

> You were chosen to be an officer because you have the potential qualities of a leader, just as an athlete is "signed" by a big league team and the aviation cadet is selected for flying training because they have certain innate abilities.
>
> **—Air Force Manual (AFM) 35-15, *Air Force Leadership* (1948)**

---

[13] 5 U.S.C. §3331, 10 U.S.C. §502.
[14] For a thorough analysis of officership in the United States military, see *The Armed Forces Officer*, National Defense University Press, 2007.

> *The function of command requires continuous alertness and willingness to accept changed conditions. Our commanders must exert superior leadership; they are expected to know and influence their soldiers. Exert your leadership—see that your soldiers 'think straight.' You won't have all the answers, but you can at least tell your soldiers that.*
>
> **—General H.H. "Hap" Arnold, from Army Air Force Letter 35-280, 19 September 1945**

Within the Air Force, only an officer can command Air Force forces.[15] Command is defined as "[t]he authority that a commander in the armed forces lawfully exercises over subordinates by virtue of rank or assignment. Command includes the authority and responsibility for effectively using available resources and for planning the employment of, organizing, directing, coordinating, and controlling military forces for the accomplishment of assigned missions. It also includes responsibility for health, welfare, morale, and discipline of assigned personnel."[16] To command, an officer is educated in the Airman's perspective and trained in Air Force capabilities. This training and perspective, combined with years of experience, produce an individual able to accept the responsibility of sending Airmen into harm's way, the sole purview of a commander.

Federal law states that commanders in the Air Force are required to be good examples of virtue, honor, patriotism, and subordination; to be vigilant in "inspecting the conduct of all persons who are placed under their command;" to guard against "dissolute and immoral practices" and correct those guilty of them; and to promote and safeguard the morale, well-being, and general welfare of the officers and enlisted personnel under their command.[17] Such tasks are sufficiently daunting that it behooves a commander to take advantage of the expertise available to him or her in an organization, informally known as a command team. The command team can consist of formal and informal members critical to maintaining the good order and discipline of an Air Force unit. The members of the command team should possess the experience, functional prowess, and maturity required to make decisions of great impact to the organization, the individuals in the organization, and the Air Force. Operating together, a commander with his or her command team leads Air Force organizations in the execution of Air Force duties.

Enlisted Members

> Commanders depend upon NCOs to lead subordinates to accomplish the mission.
>
> **—Air Force Pamphlet (AFPAM) 36-2241 (1 Jul 09), para 10.1**

---

[15] The ultimate source for command authority is the U.S. Constitution, Article II, §2, making the President the Commander-in-Chief of the US military. For military discipline purposes, 10 U.S.C. §801 states, "The term 'commanding officer' includes only commissioned officers."
[16] Joint Publication (JP) 1-02
[17] 10 U.S.C. §8583.

The Air Force's enlisted members provide the Service with the highest degree of technical expertise within their respective functional areas. Inherent in the oath of enlistment (see Appendix A), enlisted members are bound to the ideal of followership. Although not commissioned and thereby not entitled to be in command positions, enlisted members perform leadership roles across all Air Force organizational levels and are highly respected members of the Air Force leadership team. Education, training, and an Airman's perspective, combined with a wealth of technical expertise, sustain enlisted members in the leadership of other enlisted forces who support their unit, the unit's mission, and the Air Force at large.[18]

> *Throughout my Air Force career, I've seen how our Airmen demonstrate their commitment to serve—every day, around the world.*
>
> **—Chief Master Sergeant of the Air Force James A. Roy, 2009**

The Air Force enlisted members are true to a professional calling that encompasses a high degree of specialized training, Service orientation, and a distinct subculture. Enlisted members demonstrate dedication to this calling through hard work, loyalty, and mission accomplishment regardless of hardship or adversity. Often referred to as the "backbone" of the Air Force, enlisted members are grounded in the Air Force core values and are bound to the idea of followership. Enlisted members are also brought up with an Airman's perspective and receive professional military education and training tailored to appropriate levels of leadership and responsibility in accordance with AFI 36-2618, *The Enlisted Force Structure*; this document provides guidance and direction for all enlisted ranks. Enlisted members are Airmen first and specialists second. Lastly, they carry a strong belief in setting aside their own wants and needs in seeking the greatest good for their subordinates, peers, and leaders in defense of the Constitution of the United States and the officers appointed over them.

Civilians

> *If it is a military requirement, then the military will do it—if not, then you definitely want civilians doing it.*
>
> **— Roger M. Blanchard, Assistant Deputy Chief of Staff for Personnel, Headquarters Air Force, 1997-2007**

DAF civilians are indispensable to the management and operation of the Service. As civilians, they cannot exercise command authority over military members[19] but do

---

[18] See AFPAM 36-2241, Chapter 10, for a discussion on leadership and followership for the enlisted force.
[19] There are two exceptions to civilians being prohibited from commanding military forces: The President, as Commander-in-Chief under Article II, §2 of the US Constitution. In addition, 10 U.S.C. §113 and 50 U.S.C. §401 place the military departments under the direction, authority, and control of the Secretary of Defense.

perform in leadership roles throughout the Service and across all organizational levels. As of 2010, the US Air Force employs over 170,000 civilians in a full range of occupations. Civilians often provide stability and continuity as their duties and positions will frequently remain in an organization for long durations with the ability to support multiple commanders over years of service. They fill positions in staff and base sustainment operations that would otherwise be filled by military personnel. Their leadership skills are enhanced through an education and training regimen suited for their growth in the functional areas in which they provide expertise.[20] Their experiences, often honed through many years in a given functional area, give them a level of knowledge developed to an extensive degree. As stated in the Oath of Office, civilians are to understand and value the essential role of followership in mission accomplishment.

DAF civilians respond to the needs of the Air Force across the range of military operations. As an example, the Civilian Expeditionary Workforce initiative is designed to enhance the number of civilians augmenting operational requirements in contingency operations.

Former President George H. W. Bush proclaimed December 4, 1991 as "Federal Civilian Employees Remembrance Day." This recognition was bestowed upon Federal civilian employees because of the manner in which they responded to rescue and reconstruction missions with distinction and valor during the bombing of Pearl Harbor. Department of Defense civilian employees made vital contributions to the Allied war effort by performing critical administrative and technical duties in support of military operations.

—Information derived from Proclamation 6387;
Federal Civilian Employees Remembrance Day, 1991

Followership

Followership is as vital to the Air Force as is the status of an individual as an Airman. It is implicit in the duties of all officers and DAF civilians, and explicit for the enlisted force. The oath of enlistment's language makes followership a necessity of service: "…and that I will obey the orders of the President of the United States and the orders of the officers appointed over me according to regulations and the Uniform Code of Military Justice."[21] All Airmen are followers as well as leaders. The followership qualities outlined below distinguish an effective from an ineffective follower: [22]

---

[20]Air Force Policy Directive (AFPD) 36-26, *Total Force Development*, addresses how to create a total force, including DAF civilians, "successfully prepared to accomplish the Air Force mission and to lead in a rapidly evolving global environment with a vast range of missions, balancing individual needs – personal and professional – to the greatest extent possible consistent with mission accomplishment."
[21] 10 U.S.C. §502.
[22] Kelley, Robert E. "In Praise of Followers." In *Military Leadership: In Pursuit of Excellence*, 3rd Ed. Edited by Robert L. Taylor and William E. Rosenbach, Boulder: Westview Press, 1996, 136.

- ○ Self-management

- ○ Commitment

- ○ Competence

- ○ Courage

Effective followers are "…intent on high performance and recognize they share the responsibility for the quality of the relationship they have with their leaders…they know they cannot be fully effective unless they work in partnerships that require both a commitment to high performance and a commitment to develop effective relationships with partners (including their boss) whose collaboration is essential to success in their own work."[23]

Core values make the military what it is; without them, we cannot succeed. They are the values that instill confidence, earn lasting respect and create willing followers. They are the values that anchor resolve in the most difficult situations. They are the values that buttress mental and physical courage when we enter combat. In essence, they are the three pillars of professionalism that provide the foundation for military leadership at every level.

—Dr. Sheila Widnall, SECAF, 1993-1997

Research reveals specific follower attributes that produce the most effective personnel. A follower should exhibit loyalty that incorporates a high organizational commitment, a loyalty to the senior person's vision and priorities, a willingness to disagree in an appropriate and polite manner, and an ability to align personal goals with organizational ones. A follower should function well in a change-oriented environment where the person can be an agent for change and be agile in moving between the roles of leader and follower. A follower should function well on teams, collaborating with others, sharing credit, and acting responsibly toward others. A follower should exercise independent critical thinking, be willing to express courageous dissent, take the initiative in tasks, and self-manage rather than wait for guidance. A follower should ensure the core value of integrity is paramount, being trustworthy and truthful, setting and maintaining the highest performance standards, and admitting to mistakes where appropriate.[24]

---

[23] Potter, Earl H., William E. Rosenbach, Thane S. Pittman, "Leading the New Professional." In Taylor and Rosenbach, 148.

[24] Latour, Lt Col Sharon, USAF, and Lt Col Vicki Rast, USAF, "Dynamic Followership: The Prerequisite for Effective Leadership," *Air & Space Power Journal*, Winter, 2004.

Follower development is a leadership responsibility, and willingness to move out of one's comfort zone is fully expected of tomorrow's leader.[25] As loyalty is an essential quality of followership, the return loyalty of the leader is a necessary leadership quality.

THE AIR FORCE CORE VALUES

Core Values help those who join us to understand right from the outset what's expected of them. Equally important, they provide all of us, from [the rank of] Airman to four-star general, with a touchstone—a guide in our own conscience—to remind us of what we expect from ourselves. We have wonderful people in the Air Force. But we aren't perfect. Frequent reflection on the core values helps each of us refocus on the person we want to be and the example we want to set.

—General Michael E. Ryan, Chief of Staff, United States Air Force (CSAF), 1997-2001

The core values are a statement of those institutional values and principles of conduct that provide the moral framework for military activities. The professional Air Force ethic consists of three fundamental and enduring values of integrity first, service before self, and excellence in all we do.[26] This ethic is the set of values that guides the way Airmen live and perform. Success hinges on the incorporation of these values into the character of every Airman. In today's time-compressed, dynamic, and dangerous operational environment, an Airman does not have the luxury of examining each issue at leisure. He or she must fully internalize these values in order to be better prepared in all situations—to maintain integrity, to serve others before self, to perform with excellence and to encourage others to do the same. The Air Force core values—**integrity first, service before self, and excellence in all we do**—are a commitment each Airman makes when joining the Air Force. These values provide a foundation for leadership, decision-making, and success, no matter the level of an Airman's assignment, the difficulty of the task at hand, or the dangers presented by the mission.

There are four reasons the Service recognizes the Air Force core values as fundamental to its people:[27]

---

[25] Ibid.

[26] The Air Force core values were originally released in the 1997 *Air Force Core Values Handbook* (the "little blue book"). Text follows the basic structure of this handbook.

[27] Adapted from the *Air Force Core Values Handbook* (1997), Chapter II.

- ✪ **The core values tell us the price of admission to the Air Force itself.** All Air Force personnel must possess integrity first. At the same time, a person's "self" must take a back seat to Air Force service: rules must be acknowledged and followed faithfully; other personnel must be respected as persons of fundamental worth; discipline and self-control must be demonstrated always; and there must be faith in the system. In other words, the price of admission to the Air Force demands that each of us places service before self. And it is imperative that we seek excellence in all we do—whether the form is product/service excellence, resources excellence, community excellence, or operations excellence.

- ✪ **They point to what is universal and unchanging in the profession of arms.** The values are road signs inviting us to consider key features of the requirements of professional service, but they cannot hope to point to or pick out everything. By examining integrity, service, and excellence, we also eventually discover the importance of duty, honor, country, dedication, fidelity, competence, and a host of other professional requirements and attributes.

- ✪ **They help us get a fix on the ethical climate of an organization.** Big ticket scandals grow out of a climate of ethical erosion. Because some believe our operating procedures or the requirements levied upon them from above are absurd, they tend to "cut corners" or "skate by." As time goes by, these actions become easier and they become habitual until the person can no longer distinguish between the "important" taskings or rules and the "stupid" ones. Lying on official forms becomes second nature. Placing personal interests ahead of the mission becomes a natural response. And they develop a "good enough for government work" mentality. In such a climate of corrosion the core values can bring a person back to recognition of what is important: integrity, service, and excellence.

- ✪ **They serve as beacons vectoring us back to the path of professional conduct.** Adherence to the core values ensures the Air Force will not degrade from a climate of ethical commitment into a climate of corrosion.

Integrity First

Integrity is the willingness to do what is right even when no one else is looking. It is the "moral compass"—the inner voice, the voice of self-control, the basis for the trust imperative in today's Air Force.

Integrity is the single most important part of character. It makes Airmen who they are and what they stand for, and is as much a part of their professional reputation as their ability to fly or fix jets, operate a computer network, repair a runway, or defend an airbase. Airmen must be professional, both in and out of uniform. Integrity is not a suit that can be taken off at night or on the weekend or worn only when it is important to look good. Instead, it is the time that we least expect to be tested when possessing integrity is critical. People are watching us, not to see us fail, but to see us live up to their expectations. Anything less risks putting the heritage and reputation of the Air Force in peril.

Quotations from the Air Force Memorial in Washington, DC

Integrity; a man's word is his bond.

**—General Jimmy Doolittle,
US Army Air Forces Leader of the WWII Tokyo Raid**

Integrity is the fundamental premise of service in a free society. Without integrity, the moral pillars of our military strength—public trust and self-respect—are lost.

—General Charles Gabriel, 11th CSAF

We're entrusted with the security of our nation. The tools of our trade are lethal, and we engage in operations that involve risk to human life and untold national treasure. Because of what we do, our standards must be higher than those of society at large.

—General Ronald R. Fogleman, 15th CSAF

There will be demands upon your ability, upon your endurance, upon your disposition, upon your patience…just as fire tempers iron into fine steel so does adversity temper one's character into firmness, tolerance and determination.

**—Senator Margaret Chase Smith, Lieutenant Colonel,
US Air Force Reserve**

Integrity is the adherence to a strong moral code and consistency in one's actions and values. A person of integrity acts with conviction, demonstrating appropriate self-control without acting rashly. An Airman's word is binding, and honesty is the foundation of that trust. Airmen always behave in a manner that brings credit upon themselves, their unit, the Air Force, and the profession of arms. Airmen should be guided by a deeply held sense of honor, not one of personal comfort or uncontrolled selfish appetites.

Airmen act with confidence, determination, and self-control in all they do to improve themselves and their contribution to the Air Force. They maintain proper professional relationships with subordinates, superiors, and peers as well as possess the moral courage to do what is right even if the personal cost is high. As professionals, Airmen refrain from openly displaying self-pity, discouragement, anger, frustration, or defeatism or displays that would bring discredit upon themselves or the Air Force. Airmen encourage the free flow of information within organizations and never shy from criticism. They actively seek constructive feedback from superiors, peers, and subordinates and take responsibility for their own successes and failures. A person with integrity accepts the consequences of actions taken, never accepting or seeking undue credit for the accomplishments of others. Airmen also hold each other accountable for their actions and uniformly enforce standards. They ensure that all people are treated with equal respect. Finally, Airmen comprehend the awe-inspiring task of defending the Constitution of the United States, maintaining the highest traditions of honoring the Air Force's responsibilities to the nation, and understanding the sacrifices made by others who came before them.

Service Before Self

Quotations from the Air Force Memorial in Washington, DC

I have been recognized as a hero for my ten minutes of action over Vietnam, but I am no more a hero than anyone else who has served this country.

—A1C John L. Levitow, lowest ranking Air Force Medal of Honor Recipient

Service is a willingness to sacrifice...the setting aside of personal desires, comfort, and security when the safety of the country is at stake.

—General George S. Brown, 8th CSAF and 8th Chairman, Joint Chiefs of Staff

Service before self is that virtue within us all which elevates the human spirit, compels us to reach beyond our meager selves to attach our spirit to something bigger than we are.

—General John P. Jumper, 17th CSAF

As an Air Force core value, service is not about the Air Force institution, it is about an enduring commitment and dedication of the individual Airman to the age-old military virtue of selfless dedication to duty at all times and in all circumstances. This includes putting one's life at risk if called to do so. It is a willingness to set aside one's needs and to make personal sacrifices. It is an understanding of the 24-hour-a-day commitment, accepting expeditionary deployments and assignments away from home and accomplishing the task at hand no matter the hardship. Service before self means taking the time and making the effort to properly plan and execute with precision regardless of the personal costs. Service before self is total commitment to the highest ideals of personal sacrifice in defense of the Constitution and the United States.

Further, service before self does not mean service before family. Airmen have a duty to the Service and an equally strong duty to their families. The difference is that there are times when service to the nation requires subordinating the needs of the family. It is the responsibility of the Airman to prepare and provide for his or her family when deployed or when duty requires it. Airmen understand they have a duty to fulfill the unit's mission. This includes performing to the best of one's abilities the assigned responsibilities and tasks without worrying how a career will be affected. As professionals, they exercise good judgment while performing their duties and understand that rules exist for good reason. They also understand that service before self asks us to subordinate our personal interests, attitudes, and aspirations to the greater cause and the demands it places on us. It means that Airmen place the welfare of their peers and subordinates ahead of their own personal needs or comforts.

This value also demands that each Airman keep "faith" in the system. This does not mean that we may not question what we are doing or that we will blindly follow our leaders without a second thought. It means that we place our trust in the processes, procedures, and other Airmen to get the job done and in the right way. Airmen understand that an organization can achieve excellence only when all members are encouraged to excel in a cooperative atmosphere free from fear, unlawful discrimination, sexual harassment, intimidation, hazing, or unfair treatment. In addition, Airmen understand they must be loyal to their leaders, fellow Airmen, and the Air Force institution they serve. This includes demonstrated allegiance to the Constitution and loyalty to the military chain of command and to the President and Secretary of Defense.

Excellence in All We Do

This core value demands that Airmen constantly strive to perform at their best. It is a commitment to high standards and an understanding that each Airman has been entrusted with our nation's security. Airmen understand that the Air Force mission is very complex and exists in a constantly changing world. They understand that all efforts in planning and executing airpower are designed to ensure the national security interests of the United States. Therefore, they must always strive to meet or exceed standards objectively based on mission needs and continuously search for new and innovative ways to successfully accomplish the mission. It is not only a professional obligation but a moral responsibility as well.

On a personal level, Airmen seek out and complete developmental education; work to stay in their best physical, mental, and moral shape; and continue to enhance their professional competencies. They are diligent to maintain their job skills, knowledge, and personal readiness at the highest possible levels. They understand that organizational excellence can only be achieved when its members work together to successfully reach a common goal in an atmosphere that preserves individual self-worth. No Airman wins the fight alone. Each organization should foster a culture that emphasizes a team mentality while maintaining high standards and accomplishing the mission. As stewards of the nation's resources, Airmen should aggressively protect and manage both human and material assets. The most precious resource is people, and it is each Airman's responsibility to ensure that he or she is trained, fit, focused, and ready to accomplish the mission safely and effectively.

Quotations from the Air Force Memorial in Washington, DC

The future is always decided by those who put their imagination to work, who challenge the unknown, and who are not afraid to risk failure.

—General Bernard A. Shriever, The Father and Architect of Air Force Space and Ballistic Missile Programs

The power of excellence is overwhelming. It is always in demand and nobody cares about its color.

—General Daniel 'Chappie' James, First African-American United States Air Force Four-Star General

That commitment to excellence is more than desirable; in the profession of arms, it's essential. Lives depend on the fact that we maintain high standards.

—General Michael E. Ryan, 16th CSAF

Courage and innovation form our heritage and excellence is our standard. America's Airmen - Active, Guard, and Reserve - serve as a force unmatched in our air and space.

—General T. Michael 'Buzz' Moseley, 18th CSAF

The Air Force recognizes these core values as *universal and unchanging* in the profession of arms. They provide the standards with which to evaluate the ethical climate of all Air Force organizations. Finally, when needed in the cauldron of war, they are the beacons vectoring the individual along the path of professional conduct and the highest ideals of integrity, service, and excellence.

In exemplification of the Air Force Core Values, Senior Airman Jason Cunningham performed actions during Operation ENDURING FREEDOM that earned him the thanks of a grateful nation, but at the cost of his life:

CITATION TO ACCOMPANY THE AWARD OF THE AIR FORCE CROSS

(POSTHUMOUS) TO

JASON D. CUNNINGHAM

The President of the United States of America, authorized by Title 10, Section 8742, U.S.C., awards the Air Force Cross to Senior Airman Jason D. Cunningham for extraordinary heroism in military operations against an opposing armed force while serving as a pararescueman near the village of Marzak in the Paktia Province of Afghanistan on 4 March 2002. On that proud day, Airman Cunningham was the primary Air Force Combat Search and Rescue medic assigned to a Quick Reaction Force tasked to recover two American servicemen evading capture in austere terrain occupied by massed Al Qaida and Taliban forces. Shortly before landing, his MH-47E helicopter received accurate rocket-propelled grenade and small arms fire, severely disabling the aircraft and causing it to crash land. The assault force formed a hasty defense and immediately suffered three fatalities and five critical casualties. Despite effective enemy fire, and at great risk to his own life, Airman Cunningham remained in the burning fuselage of the aircraft in order to treat the wounded. As he moved his patients to a more secure location, mortar rounds began to impact within fifty feet of his position. Disregarding this extreme danger, he continued the movement and exposed himself to enemy fire on seven separate occasions. When the second casualty collection point was also compromised, in a display of uncommon valor and gallantry, Airman Cunningham braved an intense small arms and rocket-propelled grenade attack while repositioning the critically wounded to a third collection point. Even after he was mortally wounded and quickly deteriorating, he continued to direct patient movement and transferred care to another medic. In the end, his distinct efforts led to the successful delivery of ten gravely wounded Americans to life-saving medical treatment. Through his extraordinary heroism, superb airmanship, aggressiveness in the face of the enemy, and in the dedication of his service to his country, Senior Airman Cunningham reflected the highest credit upon himself and the United States Air Force.

WARFIGHTING AND THE PROFESSION OF ARMS

The central focus of the profession of arms is warfighting. As Airmen, we are given a special responsibility to ensure the most effective Air Force the world has ever seen flies and fights the right way. Airmen have inherited an Air Force forged through the ingenuity, courage, and strength of Airmen who preceded them. An Airman should strive to continue to provide the nation and the next generation of Airmen an equally dominant Air Force. Doing so requires Airmen to fully understand the profession of arms they have chosen, the commitment each Airman made by taking an oath, and the acceptance to abide by the Air Force core values. It is a mindset designed to build confidence and commitment necessary to shape the professional in each of us, and how we work as a team to accomplish the mission. This mindset is shaped through the expeditionary nature of the Service, especially in support of combat, humanitarian response, and disaster relief operations and the lessons learned from those operations. The Airman's Creed is a condensation of this mindset.[28] Fundamental to this mindset is the Code of Conduct for members of the Armed Forces of the United States, applicable to the nation's uniformed Airmen as warfighters, fighting in the Service which guards our country and our way of life. It grounds every American warfighter with an established standard of conduct to support him or her at all times, especially those times of greatest stress and duress. The Code of Conduct is presented at Appendix B.

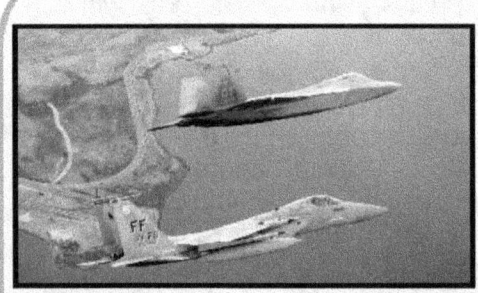

Since the Nation's birth, it has been the constitutional duty of our military to ensure national survival, defend lives and property, and promote vital interests at home and abroad. The enduring responsibility of the United States Air Force is to provide strategic deterrence for the Nation and fly, fight and win as an integral part of the Joint Team. Together with our brothers and sisters in arms, we underwrite the national strategy of defending the Homeland and assuring allies, while dissuading, deterring and defeating enemies.

—General Norton A. Schwartz, CSAF, 2008

Airmen share a long history of service, honor, and sacrifice forged in times of peace and war. From the earliest days of airpower to the heights of space to the boundless realms of cyberspace, Airmen have built an extraordinary heritage that forms the foundation of the Service's perspective. Even though we are technology focused, we value quality over quantity. We embrace change and, through transformation and innovation, we ensure a viable Air Force for the future.

Even something as straightforward as the Air Force symbol has evolved over time from the days of General Hap Arnold to the symbol we have today. It represents a sweep through our history, from a rich heritage to the horizons of the future. Through

---

[28] For insight into the reasoning behind the Airman's Creed, see the CSAF Vector, *Airman Warriors*, April 2007.

the current Air Force symbol, Airmen continue to honor the heritage of our past and build the promise of a brighter future.

Heritage to Horizon: The Air Force Symbol

Today's symbol retains the core elements of our Air Corps heritage—the Hap Arnold wings and star with circle—yet modernizes it to reflect the Air Force of today and tomorrow. The symbol has two main parts: the upper half, the stylized wings represent the stripes of our strength—the enlisted men and women of our force. They are drawn with great angularity to emphasize our swiftness and power; the lower half has a sphere, a star, and three diamonds. The sphere within the star represents the globe. It reminds each of us of our obligation to secure our nation's freedom with global vigilance, global reach, and global power. The globe also reminds us of our challenge as an expeditionary force to respond rapidly to crises and to provide decisive airpower worldwide.

The area surrounding the sphere takes the shape of a star. The star has many meanings. Its five points represent the primary components of the Total Force and family—our regular, Guard, Reserve, civilians, and retirees. The star symbolizes space as the high ground of our nation's air and space force, and as a rallying symbol in all our wars, it represents the officer corps, which is central to our combat leadership. The star is framed with three diamonds that represent the Air Force core values. Combined, the Air Force symbol presents two powerful images—at once it is an eagle (the emblem of our nation) and a medal, representing valor in service to our nation.

Airmen, firmly grounded in the core values and ingrained with a focus on the profession of arms, react to the stresses of combat, the pressures of deployed operations, and the demands of daily activities at home station with **valor**, **courage**, and **sacrifice**. While these characteristics are within each one of us, they usually come to the surface in times of great difficulty or unforeseen circumstances. Those times can happen in the workplace, on the way home from work, during a humanitarian operation, or on the battlefield. While many acts go unseen, other examples helped shape the finest traditions of the Air Force and its history. They are something not only to recognize as part of our history, but also to showcase that all Airmen may be called upon to perform above and beyond in the profession of arms.

Valor

Valor is the ability to face danger or hardship in a determined and resolute manner. It is commonly known as bravery, fearlessness, fortitude, gallantry, heart, nerve, and many other terms. Valor is the willingness to step outside of one's comfort zone to deal with an unexpected situation. Such situations can happen almost anywhere. Valor exists in places other than on the battlefield; an Airman can exhibit valor when presented with unusual circumstances in the daily routine of life. When acting with valor, one expresses heroic qualities.

Courage

Courage is about the ability to face fear, danger, or adversity. Courage primarily comes in two forms—physical and moral. Physical courage encompasses the ability to overcome fears of bodily harm to get the job done or to risk oneself for another, in battle or the course of everyday life. Moral courage is the ability to stand by the core values when confronted with difficult choices. These choices could arise from situations where unacceptable behavior (illegal drug use, sexual harassment, etc.) is condoned or ignored by certain members of an organization. They might also come from situations discovered by accident or because others are boasting of the behavior. Recognizing the behavior as inconsistent with Air Force standards should lead an Airman to inform superiors even when peer pressure exists or threats are made.

Quotations from the Air Force Memorial in Washington, DC

Courage is rightly esteemed the first of human qualities...because it is the quality which guarantees all others.

**—Sir Winston Churchill,
Prime Minister of the United Kingdom during WWII**

Courage is doing what you are afraid to do...

**—Captain Edward V. "Eddie" Rickenbacker,
Leading American Ace of WWI**

It isn't just my brother's country, or my husband's country, it's my country as well. And so the war wasn't just their war, it was my war and I needed to serve in it.

— Major Beatrice Hood Stroup, Women's Army Corps, WWII

Our nation is blessed by the courageous families who give us our courageous Airmen.

**—General David C. Jones, 9th CSAF and
9th Chairman, Joint Chiefs of Staff**

Finally, integrity breeds courage at the times and places when the behavior is most needed. More often than not, courage is shown in acts of bravery on the battlefield as Airmen step up to the challenges presented to them in a combat situation.

Sacrifice

Quotations from the Air Force Memorial in Washington, DC

They know not the day or hour nor the manner of their passing when far from home they were called to join that great band of heroic airmen that went before.

—Inscription from the American Cemetery and Memorial, Cambridge, England

…am going on a raid this afternoon…there is a possibility I won't return…do not worry about me as everyone has to leave this earth one way or another, and this is the way I have selected. If after this terrible war is over, the world emerges a saner place…pogroms and persecutions halted, then, I'm glad I gave my efforts with thousands of others for such a cause.

—Sergeant Carl Goldman, US Army Air Forces, WWII, B-17 Gunner, Killed in Action over Western Europe, from a letter to his parents

Tell them that we gave our todays for their tomorrows.

—Inscription from the Allied Cemetery, North Assam, India

…Our military families serve right alongside those of us in uniform. A special thank you to all the spouses and children and moms and dads out there praying for your loved ones in harm's way – we add our prayers, too, for their safe return.

—General Richard B. Myers, 15th Chairman, Joint Chiefs of Staff

Sacrifice entails a willingness to give up one's life, time, or comfort to meet the needs of others. Personal sacrifice can be seen on a number of levels. Most commonly, one thinks of the heroic actions of uniformed Airmen in combat with the enemy. However, day-to-day deployed garrison activities can also present opportunities to put the needs of fellow Airmen before the wants of an individual dedicated to providing excellence to the warfighter.

THE AIRMAN'S CREED

On 18 April 2007, General T. Michael Moseley, CSAF, introduced the Airman's Creed to the Air Force.[29] At that time, the Air Force had been involved in continuous combat operations for over 16 years. During that period, Airmen became highly specialized and technically capable across a broad spectrum of operations, which resulted in a drift toward an emphasis on technical proficiency and away from a warfighting orientation. As a result, General Moseley created the Airman's Creed in an effort to reinvigorate the warrior spirit and articulate the fundamental beliefs that capture the essence of the Airman warrior. The Airman's Creed is intended to remind all Airmen that they are not just a "conglomeration of diverse specialties, skill sets, or jobs," but theirs is the profession of arms. It allows Airmen to think and act with one mind, and with a commitment to fundamental warfighting beliefs. Airmen are warriors, and are dedicated to flying, fighting, and winning. Following its release, it replaced all existing Air Force-related creeds.

Tuskegee Airmen   **Doolittle Raiders**

THE AIRMAN'S CREED

I AM AN AMERICAN AIRMAN.
I AM A WARRIOR.
I HAVE ANSWERED MY NATION'S CALL.

I AM AN AMERICAN AIRMAN.
MY MISSION IS TO FLY, FIGHT, AND WIN.
I AM FAITHFUL TO A PROUD HERITAGE,
A TRADITION OF HONOR,
AND A LEGACY OF VALOR.

I AM AN AMERICAN AIRMAN,
GUARDIAN OF FREEDOM AND JUSTICE,
MY NATION'S SWORD AND SHIELD,
ITS SENTRY AND AVENGER.
I DEFEND MY COUNTRY WITH MY LIFE.

I AM AN AMERICAN AIRMAN:
WINGMAN, LEADER, WARRIOR.
I WILL NEVER LEAVE AN AIRMAN BEHIND,
I WILL NEVER FALTER,
AND I WILL NOT FAIL.

Deploying to Southwest Asia   **Training Iraqis for explosive ordnance disposal**

---

[29] "Airman's Creed Exemplifies Warfighting Ethos," http://www.af.mil/news/story.asp?id=123049390, accessed 10 Jun 09.

CHAPTER TWO

LEADING AIRMEN

I'm firmly convinced that leaders are not born; they're educated, trained, and made, as in every other profession. To ensure a strong, ready Air Force, we must always remain dedicated to this process.

—General Curtis E. LeMay, CSAF, 1961-1965

Leadership is the art and science of motivating, influencing, and directing Airmen to understand and accomplish the Air Force mission in joint warfare.[30] This highlights two fundamental elements of leadership: (1) the mission, objective, or task to be accomplished, and (2) the Airmen who accomplish it. All facets of Air Force leadership should support these two fundamental elements. Effective leadership transforms human potential into effective performance in the present and prepares capable leaders for the future.

Any Airman can be a leader and can positively influence those around him or her to accomplish the mission. Leadership does not equal command, but all commanders should be leaders.[31] The vast majority of Air Force leaders are not commanders. Individuals who have stepped forward to lead others in accomplishing the mission simultaneously serve as both leaders and followers at every level of the Air Force, from young Airmen working in aircrew flight equipment, to captains at wing staffs, to civilian

---

[30] AFM 35-15, *Air Force Leadership* (1948): "Leadership is the art of influencing people to progress with cooperation and enthusiasm toward the accomplishment of a mission." AFP 35-49, *Air Force Leadership* (1985): "Leadership is the art of influencing and directing people to accomplish the mission." The definition in the text is a distillation of these earlier efforts to define leadership for the Air Force.

[31] This concept dates back to AFM 35-15 (1948): "You can be a commander without being a leader, or you may be a fine leader without a command. But you must be a good leader to be an efficient commander" (AFM 35-15, page 4).

directors, to generals at the Pentagon. Leaders positively influence their entire organization, without necessarily being the commander.

The Air Force expects its members to develop leadership skills. The nature and extent of that development depends on the member's status: officer, enlisted, or civilian. The Air Force expects an officer to move quickly through the levels of leadership, from tactical expertise into operational competence. Many will move into the level of strategic vision.[32] Air Force enlisted members will operate chiefly at the level of tactical expertise, where their technical skills are combined with their direct influence on subordinate members. DAF civilians can function at all levels of leadership, but, with the exception of the President of the United States and authorities granted to the Secretary of Defense,[33] they can never command. The pinnacle of leadership is to command where the responsibility for making life and death decisions as well as taking organizational responsibility resides. Officers can rise to command Air Force forces or a joint force.

Followers also have a critical role in displaying loyalty, as well as core values needed to accomplish the Air Force mission. A commander should be comfortable leaving his or her unit in the hands of the next in command, without feeling the need to routinely check in to ascertain the status of the unit. If the commander has done his or her job right in developing followers who can step in with competence and confidence, no fear for the health of the unit during absence should exist.

The abilities of a leader can be improved through deliberate use of force development, built from education, training, and experience (see Chapter 3 for a full discussion of force development). All Airmen can achieve excellence by living the Air Force core values, developing institutional competencies, acquiring professional and technical competence, and then acting on such abilities to accomplish the unit's mission, while taking care of the unit's personnel. Core values permeate leadership at all levels, at all times. Leaders at the more junior levels demonstrate personal institutional competencies needed to create a cohesive unit fully supportive of its mission. Mid-level leaders use institutional competencies at the people/team level to advance the organization's responsibilities within the framework of the operational mission. The more senior the leader, the more crucial becomes his or her use of organizational competencies in effecting mission accomplishment. The ability to influence people, improve performance, and accomplish a mission—leadership actions—are part of all levels of leadership.

FOUNDATIONS OF AIR FORCE LEADERSHIP

From its inception in 1947,[34] the Air Force has recognized its distinctiveness as a Service and the importance of leadership in the accomplishment of the mission. For a

---

[32] Levels of leadership are defined more thoroughly later in this chapter.

[33] The President's authority is derived from the United States Constitution, Article II, §2. The Secretary of Defense's authority is derived from 10 U.S.C. §113 and 50 U.S.C. §401.

[34] The National Security Act of 1947 (as amended).

variety of reasons, the Air Force focus on the foundational leadership elements—people and mission—has evolved over time from an emphasis on one foundational element over the other, to today's more balanced approach.

The first effort to codify leadership for US Air Force Airmen, rather than US Army Air Force Soldiers, was Air Force Manual (AFM) 35-15 (1948); its thrust was in emphasizing the psychological aspects of leadership, taking much of its tone from a 1943 National Research Council study, *Psychology for the Fighting Man*.[35] The emphasis was on the "art" of leadership:

> The very fact that leadership is an art should discourage your becoming a mechanical leader. Leadership does not provide formulas, rules, or methods which will fit every situation. Leadership is an intangible quality which cannot be seen, felt, or measured except through its results. Moreover, you cannot predict the results with mathematical accuracy. If you have skill as a leader, however, you can predict results within the limits of your objectives.[36]

The manual emphasized seven "aspects" of leadership and discussion of them was interspersed throughout: Mission, Integrity of Character, Responsibility, Influencing Men, Knowing Men, Unity, and Morale.[37] The current definition of leadership owes much to the emphasis on the mission and the people (Mission, Influencing Men, and Knowing Men), and the current Air Force core values are foreshadowed in the other aspects (Integrity of Character, Responsibility, Unity, Morale). It also listed six "attributes of a leader:" Integrity of Character, Sense of Responsibility, Professional Ability, Energy, Emotional Stability, and Humaneness.[38] The attributes individualized the seven aspects, by applying them to the officer as a leader. The current Air Force core values trace their origins directly to these attributes.

Admittedly, the manual recognized the lessons incorporated were based on "an organization similar to a World War II air force unit composed of civilians who had to be quickly trained as soldiers."[39] It acknowledged that the future Airman will function in more intricate organizations with more complex duties, requiring the Airman to become a more "complex being whose behavior can less and less be placed within any simple pattern."[40] The entire publication focused solely on the Air Force officer. Its discussions revolved around both leadership and command for officers, with no direct information written to address the leadership concerns or challenges of the enlisted force or civilians.

---

[35] AFM 35-15, *Air Force Leadership* (1948), p. 1.
[36] Ibid.
[37] Ibid., p. 3.
[38] Ibid., pp. 48-53.
[39] Ibid., p. 2. The term "soldier" was still used to describe members of the Air Force at this time.
[40] Ibid.

In 1955, the Air Force published AFM 50-21, *Living for Leadership*. It represented a dramatic change of focus from its 1948 predecessor, with chapter titles such as Patterns for Living, Convictions for Living, and Courageous Living. Heavily illustrated, it provided insight into the culture of the day as interpreted by the Air Force for its officers. This manual was a product of its time, which emphasized Western faith and values to combat "the faith of the Communist." In the aggregate, the document is a time capsule of America, giving guidance for how to live, vice how to lead.

In 1964, the Air Force returned to AFM 35-15 form and structure with the introduction of AFM 50-3, *Air Force Leadership.* The aspects of leadership and attributes of a leader are identical to the earlier edition but focus more on the mission and place a greater urgency in deterrence and readiness. The chapter on "Mission" highlights this edition's emphasis, appropriate for its time. Then-Secretary of the Air Force (SECAF) Eugene M. Zuckert (1961-1965) was quoted to establish the overarching responsibility of the Air Force, hence the Airman's perspective at the time:

> Ours is the primary responsibility to prevent the domination of the aerospace by any power or combination of powers whose interests are inimical to freedom and national independence on Earth...Space is a medium of possible military action. As such, we must view the operating problems in space as an extension of those in the atmosphere. That is why we in the Air Force call it the aerospace.[41]

With the United States engaged in a struggle for nuclear dominance with the Soviet Union, the CSAF, General Curtis E. LeMay placed his emphasis on how Air Force officers should lead (the document continued to focus exclusively on officers): "We maintain our aerospace forces in readiness to respond to any kind of military challenge the Communists may make. We must be prepared to emerge victorious from a general war should it be forced upon us."[42] Consistent with AFM 50-3's emphasis on the mission, LeMay went on to say, "No matter how well you apply the art of leadership, no matter how strong the unit or high the morale of your men, if your leadership is not directed completely toward the execution of the mission, your leadership has failed."[43]

In 1985, the Air Force recognized the importance of balancing the people and the mission which led to the development of Air Force Pamphlet (AFP) 35-49, *Air Force Leadership*. This pamphlet simplified the Service's discussion on leadership, defining the term in succinct language: "Leadership is the art of influencing and directing people to accomplish the mission."[44] It also provided a new list of leadership traits for the Air Force, most derived at least tacitly from the leadership attributes from AFMs 35-15 and 50-3: integrity, loyalty, commitment, energy, decisiveness, and selflessness. In addition, it provided leadership principles, similar to the earlier leadership aspects: know your job, know yourself, set the example, care for people, communicate, educate,

---

[41] AFM 50-3, *Air Force Leadership* (1964), p. 10.
[42] Ibid.
[43] Ibid., p. 11.
[44] AFP 35-49, *Air Force Leadership* (1985), p. 1.

equip, motivate, accept your responsibility, and develop teamwork.[45] AFP 35-49 was "a basic guide for the new and for the aspiring Air Force leader."[46] Unique to this Air Force document on leadership was the removal of its explicit application to officers only. The document referred to all leaders, without regard to rank or command authority.

Finally, AFDD 1-1, *Leadership and Force Development*, the predecessor to this volume, was signed by General John P. Jumper, CSAF, in 2004. Aspects and attributes of leadership became core values, supported by enduring leadership competencies, which now have been updated into the Service's institutional competencies. This current version is based on that document's framework, expanded to meet the needs of today's Air Force. Figure 2.1 illustrates the evolution of leadership dimensions from attributes, to traits, to core values—*Integrity, Service, Excellence*—which now provide the underpinning for leadership in today's Air Force.

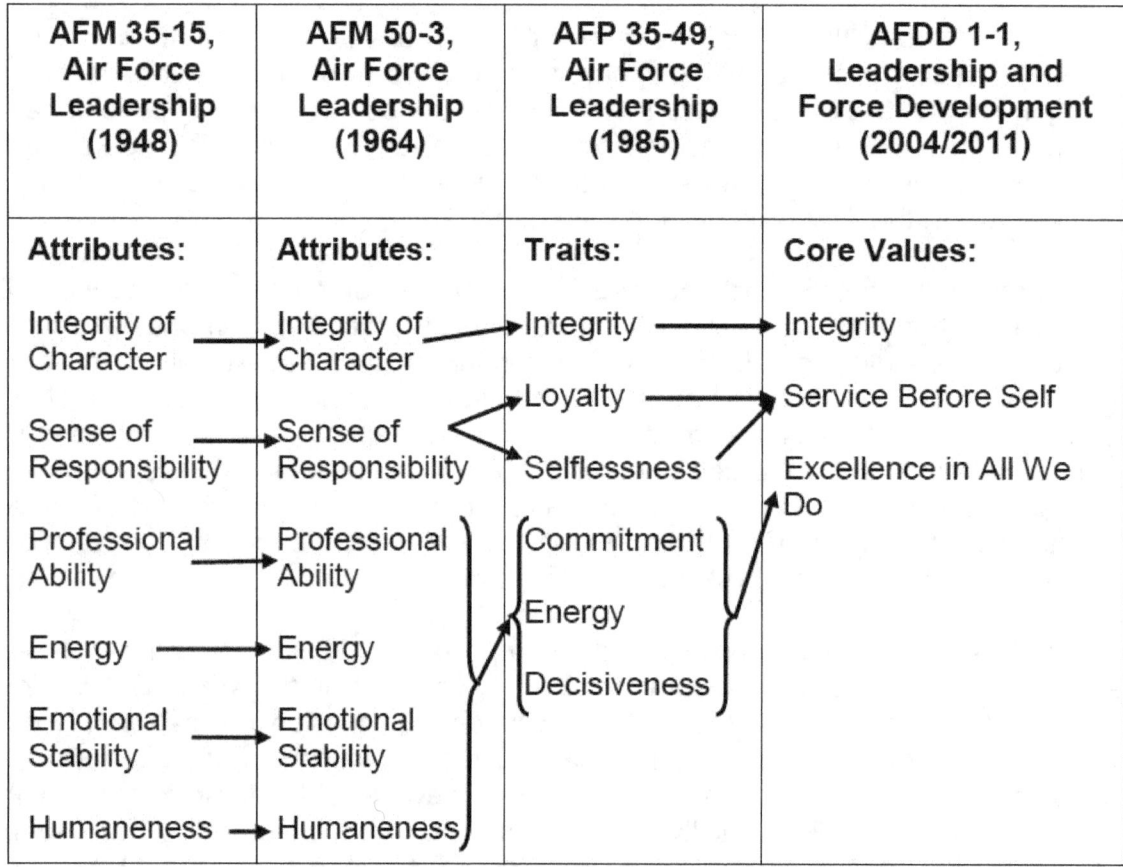

Figure 2.1. Evolution of Air Force Leadership Dimensions

---

[45] Ibid., pp. 2-5.
[46] Ibid., p. 1.

LEVELS OF AIR FORCE LEADERSHIP

A smaller force structure combined with an accelerating pace of change requires some proactive thinking about leadership development.

—General Michael E. Ryan, CSAF, 1997-2001

The Air Force operates in a dynamic global context across multiple domains requiring leadership skills at a variety of levels. The Air Force characterizes these leadership levels as the tactical expertise, operational competence, and strategic vision levels.[47] The leadership level at which an Airman operates determines the institutional competencies required to lead Airmen in mission accomplishment. As shown in Figure 2.2, as Airmen progress from the tactical expertise to strategic vision leadership levels, emphasis on the use of institutional competencies shifts from personal to organizational, with a generally consistent focus on people/team competencies.

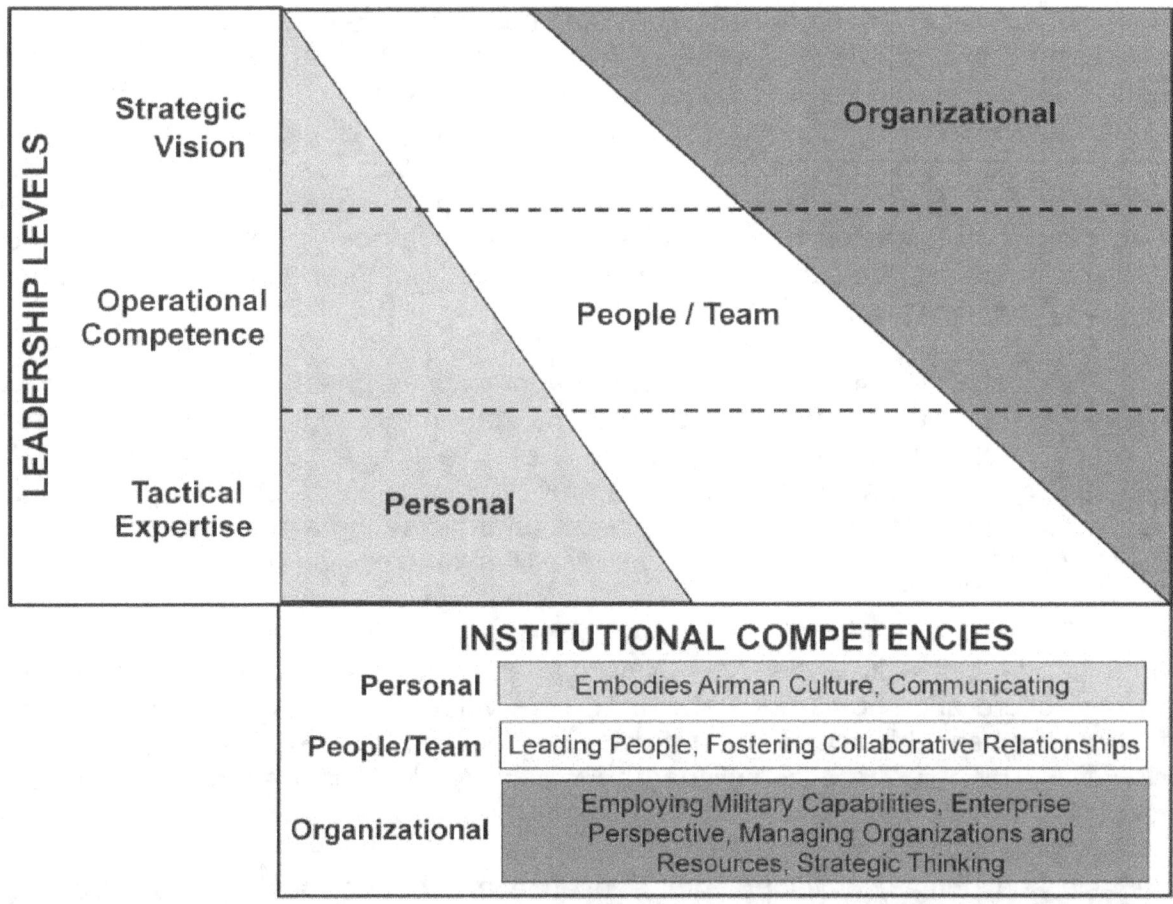

Figure 2.2. Relationship of Leadership Levels with Institutional Competencies

---

[47] Terms for the leadership levels were approved by General John P. Jumper, CSAF (2001-2005).

Tactical Expertise

I think it's important that leadership opportunities be forced to as low a commissioned level as possible. That's a good time to start looking at a guy. For heaven's sake! What can you put in his ER besides the fact that the guy is a great stick, he does well on instruments, is a good gunner, and he talked to the Kiwanis club once a quarter downtown. What else can you put in there? How do you separate the wheat from the chaff? Get him in a leadership role!

—General Hoyt S. Vandenberg
CSAF, 1948-1953

Personal competencies are the primary focus at the tactical expertise level. Airmen are also gaining a general understanding of team leadership and an appreciation for organizational leadership. Airmen at this level master their core duty skills, develop experiences in applying those skills, and begin to acquire the knowledge and experience that will produce the qualities essential to effective leadership. Airmen at the tactical expertise level are the Air Force's technicians and specialists. They learn about themselves as leaders and how their leadership acumen can affect others through the use of ethical leadership. They are being assimilated into the Air Force culture and are adopting the core values of our Service. Airmen at this level are focused on honing followership abilities, motivating subordinates and influencing peers to accomplish the mission while developing a warrior ethos. They are learning about themselves and their impact on others in roles as both follower and leader in addition to developing their communication skills.

Tactical expertise in the Air Force encompasses chiefly the unit and sub-unit levels where individuals perform specific tasks that, in the aggregate, contribute to the execution of operations at the operational level. Tactical expertise includes activities such as flying an aircraft, guarding a perimeter, loading a pallet, setting up a firewall for a base, identifying a potentially hostile radar return, treating a broken arm, and many other forms of activity, accomplished by both military and civilian personnel.

Training and education at the tactical level includes training in a primary skill and initial education in leadership. New Airmen should be educated in the common Service culture and should understand the core values that bond Airmen together. In addition, they should receive an understanding of, and gain expertise in, their unique specialty. This may be accomplished by the following tactical education and training activities:

✪ Basic and primary developmental education and undergraduate academic degree programs

✪ Specialty training

✪ Continuation training

The following examples illustrate use of the above activities: Junior enlisted Airmen will complete basic training for indoctrination into Air Force culture, attend the relevant technical schools to obtain the occupational skills needed for their duties, and then receive orientation into their new organization at the local First Term Airman Center. As they gain experience and advance within their units, they will attend Airman Leadership School to enhance their ability to function as leaders within their organizations. Similarly, recently commissioned officers will obtain indoctrination to the Air Force through their commissioning sources, then receive the appropriate technical training, followed by completion of the Air and Space Basic Course. After several years of practical experience in their initial assignments, they will receive further leadership education through Squadron Officer School. Air Force civilian members may similarly attend these or comparable civilian education courses. Throughout this time, Airmen gain experience in their specific duties through daily performance, making them more competent and qualified to accomplish their assigned missions. Throughout these education and training events, individuals are assessed to monitor their progress. Mentoring by those senior to these Airmen and civilians is vital to their progress in the Air Force.

Effective commanders and supervisors find the proper balance of training, education, and leadership opportunities to develop the tactical competence of their Airmen. They should work closely with educators and trainers and follow the guiding principles of the personal institutional competencies when developing their Airmen at the tactical level.

The leadership study, "Security Police Defense of Tan Son Nhut and Bien Hoa Air Bases, January 1968," in Appendix E is provided to present tactical expertise in a concrete and demonstrable setting.

Operational Competence

The full-spectrum of institutional competencies is balanced across the operational competence leadership level. At this level, Airmen are able to understand the broader Air Force perspective and the integration of diverse people and their capabilities in the execution of operations. This level is where an Air Force member transitions from being a specialist to understanding Air Force operational capabilities. Based on a thorough understanding of themselves as leaders and followers and how they influence others, they apply an understanding of organizational and team dynamics. They continue to develop personal leadership skills, while developing their people/team competencies. The operational level includes continued broadening of experience.

Leading people through developing and inspiring others, taking care of people, and taking advantage of the diversity in the ranks of followers is vital to this level of leadership.[48]   Also at this level, fostering collaborative relationships through building teams and coalitions, especially within a large organization, and negotiating with others, often external to the organization, becomes a necessary competence.   Airmen operating at this level of leadership normally assume such responsibilities following intermediate developmental education. The focus of Air Force organization and employment is at the operational level. It is here where warfighting is executed and day-to-day command and control of Air Force operations are carried out. At this level, the tactical skills and expertise Airmen developed earlier are employed alongside new leadership opportunities to affect an entire theater or joint operations area. By now the Airman has developed a family of skills at both the personal and people/team level, grounded in the Airman's perspective and guided by ingrained core values.

Education and training at the operational level allow Airmen to integrate expertise to produce operational effects for Air Force missions. At this level, education assumes a larger role in an Airman's development. Intermediate developmental education is intended to enhance professional competence. Operational-level education focuses on furthering expertise across related specialties and increasing leadership responsibilities. Operational-level training continues to build tactical skills and develops professional competence.

(General Carl) Spaatz possessed a good measure of (a) necessary ingredient of a successful general—the ability to inspire trust in both superiors and subordinates. His chief lieutenant, Jimmy Doolittle, in an oral-history interview with Ronald R. Fogleman, then a major, stated, "I idolize General Spaatz. He is perhaps the only man that I have ever been closely associated with whom I have never known to make a bad decision." This praise, coming from a man of enormous physical and moral courage and high intellect, speaks for itself.

General Carl Spaatz,
First CSAF, 1947-1948

—Dr. Richard Davis, published in
***Aerospace Power Journal*, Winter 1997**

Operational education, training, and experience may consist of:

○ Intermediate developmental education.

○ Joint professional military education.

○ Professional continuing education programs.

○ Advanced academic degree programs.

○ Education with industry.

---

[48] For additional information on diversity in the Air Force, see AFPD 36-70, *Diversity*.

- Fellowships.
- Specialty schools/advanced training.
- Experience through career broadening assignments within the Air Force.
- Training through assignments at the major command or combatant command level.

The following examples describe elements of operational competence: Majors will be expected to perform duties as flight commanders or operations officers to gain skills at a higher level in the squadron and complete intermediate developmental education or a selected graduate-level degree program to further their learning as maturing professionals. Noncommissioned officers attend the Noncommissioned Officers Academy and relevant specialty schools, and pursue professional continuing education programs. Civilian personnel at this level fill positions with greater organizational and technical responsibilities. As with their military counterparts, they may be selected to attend an advanced academic degree program; Service schools, such as intermediate developmental education; or education with industry.

During an operation, decisions have usually to be made at once; there may be no time to review the situation or even to think it through…. If the mind is to emerge unscathed from this relentless struggle with the unforeseen, two qualities are indispensable: First, an intellect that, even in the darkest hour, retains some glimmerings of the inner light [commander's vision] which leads to truth; and second, the courage to follow this faint light wherever it may lead.

—Karl von Clausewitz, *On War*

The leadership study, "General Creech and the Transformation of Tactical Air Command," in Appendix E is provided to present operational competence in a concrete and demonstrable setting.

Strategic Vision

At this level, Airmen combine highly developed personal and people/team institutional competencies to apply broad organizational competencies. They develop a deep understanding of Air Force Service core functions and how Airmen achieve synergistic results and desired effects with their operational capabilities. They also understand how the Air Force operates within joint, multinational, and interagency relationships. At this level, an Airman's required competencies transition from the integration of people with missions to leading and directing exceptionally complex and multi-tiered organizations.

At this level of leadership, an Airman employs military capabilities, applying the operational and strategic arts with a thorough understanding of capabilities of units, the Air Force at large, and joint and coalition forces. The Airman with strategic vision has an enterprise perspective, with a comprehension of the structure and relationships in the overall enterprise with which he or she is involved. This perspective requires an awareness of the processes of our government and of the global, regional, and cultural issues surrounding a given mission. Strategic thinking is imperative at this level, emphasizing the need for a broad vision and adaptability to circumstances for which earlier leadership challenges in his or her career have prepared the Airman. Managing organizations and resources become more significant to exercising leadership at this level.

Hindenburg looked back to Hannibal's Battle of Cannae, and made his disposition to fight the Russians at Tannenberg. Napoleon studied the campaigns of Alexander the Great and Genghis Khan, the Mongol. The navies draw their inspiration from the Battle at Actium in the time of the Romans, and the sea fight of Trafalgar. In the development of airpower, one has to look ahead and not backward, and figure out what is going to happen, not too much what has happened. That is why the older services have been psychologically unfit to develop this new arm to the fullest extent practicable with the methods and means at hand.

—Brigadier General Billy Mitchell

The level of strategic vision includes challenges to gain breadth of experience and leadership perspective (e.g., educational opportunities; training focused on the institutional Air Force; joint, intergovernmental, business, and international views). Senior developmental education strengthens an Airman's grasp of the complexities required to operate at this level of leadership. Strategic vision focuses on the effects an Airman can have across a major command, a theater, the Air Force, or even other Services or the Department of Defense. A commander of Air Force forces dual-hatted as a joint force air component commander, the Chief Master Sergeant of the Air Force, or a Senior Executive Service civilian responsible for Service personnel policies operate at this level. Senior leaders need strategic comprehension and competence, as well as broad perspectives and the ability to effectively lead in an expeditionary environment. At the strategic level of leadership, Airmen receive further opportunities to expand their breadth of experience and have the greatest ability to impact and support the Air Force's role in military operations.[49]

The greatest lesson of this war has been the extent to which air, land, and sea operations can and must be coordinated by joint planning and unified command.

—General Henry H. "Hap" Arnold

Education, training, and experience at the strategic vision level help develop the skills to form accurate frames of reference, make sound decisions, uncover underlying connections to deal with more challenging issues, and engage in creative, innovative thinking that recognizes new solutions and new options. At this level, education assumes a predominant role in an Airman's development. Education emphasizes understanding of broad concepts and offers insights into complex issues not commonly available in operational environments. It focuses on the institutional Air Force and joint, interagency, business, and international views. Exercises and wargames provide opportunities to validate training and education. Development at the strategic level is commonly presented through:

○ Senior developmental education.

○ Operational assignments.

○ Exercises and wargames.

○ Self-development.

○ Mentoring.

---

[49] Policy guidance on force development through the leadership levels can be found in AFI 36-2640, *Executing Total Force Development,* and AFI 36-2618, *The Enlisted Force Structure.*

At the strategic vision level, assignment to senior command (for officers) or staff (for all Airmen) duties in both Service and joint or coalition organizations round out the skills of the Airman through experiential growth. Senior developmental education programs, such as Air War College or the Senior Noncommissioned Officer Academy, improve breadth of professional development.

The leadership study, "Strategic Noncommissioned Officer Leadership and Establishing a Strategic Vision for the Enlisted Force," in Appendix E is provided to present strategic vision in a concrete and demonstrable setting.

LEADERSHIP COMPONENTS

Good leaders are people who have a passion to succeed.... To become successful leaders, we must first learn that no matter how good the technology or how shiny the equipment, people-to-people relations get things done in our organizations. People are the assets that determine our success or failure. If you are to be a good leader, you have to cultivate your skills in the arena of personal relations.

**—General Ronald R. Fogleman,
CSAF, 1994-1997**

In the Air Force, leadership is comprised of two main components: institutional competencies and leadership actions. These are intrinsic to all Airmen, building on the foundation laid by the core values. Leaders apply these components at all three leadership levels: tactical expertise, operational competence, and strategic vision.

Institutional Competencies

The nature and scope of leadership challenges, as well as the methods by which leadership is exercised, differ based on the level of leadership and responsibility. Leadership at the tactical level is predominantly direct and face-to-face, first exercised at the junior officer and noncommissioned officer levels. As leaders ascend the organizational ladder to the operational level, leadership tasks become more complex and sophisticated, accomplished most regularly at the field grade officer and senior noncommissioned officer levels. Strategic leaders have responsibility for large organizations or systems, and deal with issues requiring more interorganizational cooperation and longer timelines. Senior officers, routinely at the general officer rank, the most senior enlisted personnel, and civilians in the Senior Executive Service perform most often at this level.

As leaders move through successively higher echelons in the Air Force, they need a wider portfolio of competencies, those typically gained at previous levels of leadership. As military and civilian leaders progress within the Air Force, they serve in more complex and interdependent organizations, have increased personal responsibility and authority, and require significantly different competencies than their subordinates. As leaders advance into the most complex and highest levels of the Air Force or become involved in the strategic arena, the ability to conceptualize and integrate becomes increasingly important. Leaders at this level focus on establishing the fundamental conditions for operations to deter wars, fight wars, or conduct operations other than war. They also create organizational structures needed to deal with future requirements.

The personal competencies are among the first taught to new Airmen; for example, they are key elements of officer and enlisted accession training. While personnel at all levels of leadership use these competencies to varying degrees, company grade officers and junior to mid-ranking enlisted members most extensively use them. Curricula for the Noncommissioned Officer Academy and Squadron Officer College emphasize the importance of personal competencies. The people/team competencies are emphasized more for field grade officers and senior noncommissioned officers. Intermediate developmental education, such as Air Command and Staff College or the Senior Noncommissioned Officer Academy, places great stock in the education of these competencies. Senior developmental education, such as Air War College and the Chief Master Sergeant Leadership Course, is the provenance of organizational competencies.

Leadership Actions

You don't lead by hitting people over the head—that's assault, not leadership.

—President Dwight David Eisenhower

Air Force leaders act in a decisive manner to **influence** their subordinates through techniques that include communication, motivation, and setting of standards. The result is a unit able to effectively perform a mission. Air Force leaders also **improve** their unit's abilities through development via education, training, and experience. The result is an enhanced ability to **accomplish** the unit's assigned missions. Leaders influence and improve their units in order to accomplish their military mission.

○ **Influence.** Leaders motivate and inspire people by creating a vision of a desirable end-state and keeping them moving in the right direction to achieve that vision. To do this, leaders tailor their behavior toward their fellow Airmen's need for motivation, achievement, sense of belonging, recognition, self-esteem, and control over their lives.

○ **Improve.** Leaders foster growth by insisting that their people focus attention on the aspects of a situation, mission, or project they control. Challenge should be an integral part of every job; for people to learn and excel, they must be motivated. Leaders should provide challenging and enlightening experiences. It is important to identify and analyze success to make the underlying causes and behaviors permanent and pervasive, not temporary and specific. Leaders encourage the learning process by formally recognizing individual and unit success, no matter how large or small. Leaders create more leaders.

○ **Accomplish.** Air Force leaders influence people, improve their abilities, and direct their activities to accomplish their military mission. Leaders ensure the effects that successfully achieve desired objectives.

CHAPTER THREE

FORCE DEVELOPMENT

> *Force Development will enable us to focus on each individual by emphasizing our common Airman culture.... Every aspect of Force Development has one common goal: To continue developing professional Airmen who instinctively leverage their respective strengths together. We intend to develop leaders who motivate teams, mentor subordinates, and train successors.*
>
> **—General John P. Jumper, CSAF, 2001-2005**

People are the Air Force's most critical asset. Airmen turn competencies into required capabilities. For this reason, the art of employing Airmen with the requisite education, training, and experience is fundamental to the effectiveness of the Service, affecting current operations and future capabilities. **Force development is a deliberate process of preparing Airmen through the continuum of learning (CoL) with the required competencies to meet the challenges of the 21st Century.** The CoL is a career-long process of individual development where challenging experiences are combined with education and training through a common taxonomy to produce Airmen who possess the tactical expertise, operational competence, and strategic vision to lead and execute the full spectrum of Air Force missions.[50] The CoL is implemented through institutional competencies, as delineated in the institutional competency (IC) list (see Appendix C). Institutional competencies are measurable clusters of skills, knowledge, and abilities required of all Airmen and are needed to operate successfully in a constantly changing environment. They are presented in this document as the underpinning concepts for force development. Occupational competencies support the overarching institutional competencies and are associated with a particular function or career field; they are found in supporting directives for those functions and career fields. Common guiding principles for education, training, and experience provide a basis for the development of Airmen into leaders and show how institutional competencies are used in the Air Force.

FORCE DEVELOPMENT CONSTRUCT

The Air Force has been successful in producing leaders. However, the evolution of technology and the dynamic global security environment demand a leadership

---

[50] Definition established in this document, based on policies and research in AFPD 36-26, *Total Force Development*; AFI 36-2640, *Executing Total Force Development*; AFI 36-2618, *The Enlisted Force Structure*; and AF/A1D Strategic Plan Implementation: Goal 3, Force Development Synchronization Initiative, 18 December 2006.

development approach that keeps pace. The Air Force requires a direct, deliberate development philosophy that prepares Airmen to meet warfighter requirements. The force development construct of the Air Force provides such direction.

Force development is a function of both individual and Air Force institutional responsibility. All Airmen have a responsibility to take advantage of and enhance their education and training, while the institution is responsible for providing the opportunity for each Airman to do so. Force development provides a leadership focus at all levels of an Airman's career through a repetitive process of development involving education, training, and experience, seasoned with ongoing mentoring by more experienced Airmen.

Success of Air Force operations depends on the effective integration of human capabilities with the tools, tactics, techniques, and procedures that combine to produce the full spectrum of airpower. The first steps in integrating people into Air Force operations are defining the required capabilities, then organizing the competencies and skill sets required to produce those capabilities.

The goal of force development is to link the Airman's perspective with defined competencies and processes to prepare Airmen to successfully lead and act in the midst of rapidly evolving requirements, while attempting to meet both their personal and professional expectations.

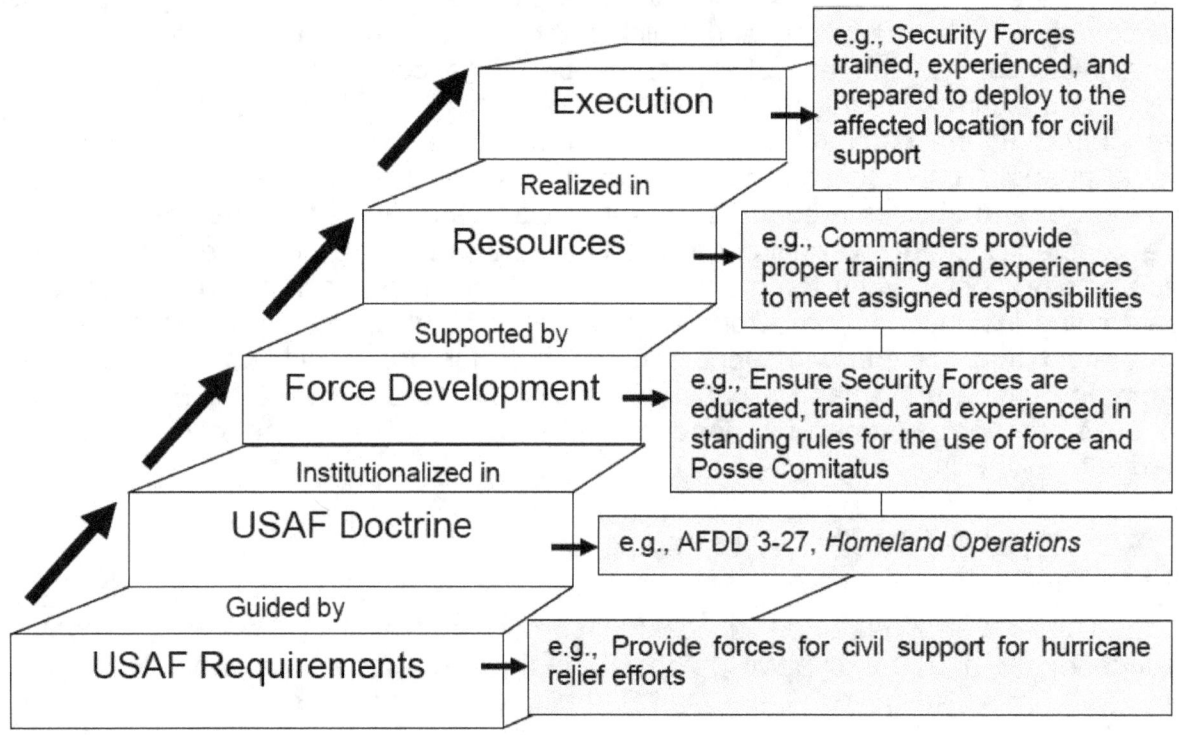

Figure 3.1. Force Development Construct in Application

The need for Airmen who possess the right occupational skills and institutional competencies forms the core requirement of force development and is the basis for all force development efforts. The construct, as depicted in Figure 3.1, starts with understanding mission requirements and translating them into capabilities. These requirements derive ultimately from the National Security and National Military Strategies. Doctrine identifies the best practices of the Air Force that it brings to all operations, within which force development is used to create leaders and commanders. Doctrine guides the presentation and employment of Air Force capabilities. The result of the process is execution of the mission by the Airman, prepared to perform as required.

THE CONTINUUM OF LEARNING

The deliberate process of combining education, training, and experience to produce the right expertise and competence to meet the Air Force's operational needs is the key element of developing an Airman. The CoL focuses on developing Airmen who thoroughly understand the mission, the organization, and Air Force doctrine. These complementary aspects of force development are essential in tailoring the right development to the right person at the right time. This is an ongoing process, continuously being examined for new needs.

Education, training, and experience are the components of the CoL. Education and training represent a large investment of resources and are the primary tools in developing Airmen. They apply to the development of Airmen at all leadership levels. Education, training, and experience are distinct but related force development activities.

> **Bottom Line:**
>
> **Force Development leverages education, training, and experience to produce adaptable, creative, knowledgeable Airmen.**

Education provides critical thinking skills, encouraging exploration into unknown areas and creative problem solving. Its greatest benefit comes in unknown situations or new challenges; education prepares the individual for unpredictable scenarios. Conversely, training is focused on a structured skill set, and the results of training performance should be consistent. Thus, training provides the individual with skill expertise. Education and training together provide the tools for developing Airmen. For a further discussion on the differences between education and training, see Appendix D. Experience, the continuously growing part of any Airman's career, is where the synthesis of education and training occurs.

The Air Force believes in learning along the entire timeline or continuum of an Airman's service, beginning with the learning obtained from accession sources, and continuing throughout a career. Over the course of service in the Air Force, each Airman will have the opportunity to be a leader. Through the CoL, the Air Force exposes Airmen to a broad-based education, training, and experience framework that equips them with the competencies to serve as leaders as they progress in rank and responsibility.

INSTITUTIONAL COMPETENCIES

> *Use of a common competency language promotes a common understanding of the key elements of each job and the capabilities resident in the workforce, which enables identification of critical gaps and potential solutions within the force.*
>
> **— Lt Gen Richard Y. Newton III**
> **DCS, Manpower & Personnel, 2009**

Core values are the ultimate starting point for service. Airmen subsequently require a means to build their capabilities that will support the needs of the Air Force. These means are known as competencies. To develop the capabilities of Airmen, the Air Force uses a systematic competency-based approach to develop a force capable of providing decisive effects, integrate the total force, and increase the agility of the Service.

Competencies are attributes an individual possesses to successfully and consistently perform a given task, under specified conditions, or meeting a defined standard of performance. This enables Airmen to perform their jobs and contribute to the overall success of the Air Force. Competencies influence human performance and have a subsequent impact on mission and organizational success.

Institutional competencies prepare Airmen to operate successfully across the widest array of Air Force tasks and requirements. These competencies provide a common language and a set of priorities for consistency across the Air Force. The Air Force's institutional competencies are key to ensuring the ability of Airmen to operate successfully in a constantly changing operational environment. They are broadly applicable and span all occupations, functions, and organizational levels. These competencies place the institutional responsibilities into a context of how the individual should be developed and form the framework for force development in the Air Force. The institutional competency list consists of 8 competencies and 24 sub-competencies. They are grouped into three categories: personal, people/team, and organizational.

Personal competencies are those competencies needed in face-to-face and interpersonal relationships that directly influence human behavior and values. They are essential for individual contribution, for building cohesive units, and for empowering immediate subordinates.

People/Team competencies involve more interpersonal and team relationships. They represent competencies that, when combined with the personal competencies, are essential as Airmen's responsibilities are increased.

Organizational competencies represent those applicable at all levels of the Air Force but are most in demand at the strategic level. Effective organizational competency skills include technical competence on force structure and integration; on unified, joint, multinational, and interagency operations; on resource allocation; and on management of complex systems. In addition, they apply to conceptual competence in creating policy, vision, and interpersonal skills emphasizing consensus building and influencing peers and other policy makers, both internal and external to the organization.

For a full listing and explanation of each institutional competency and subcompetency, see Appendix C, Institutional Competency List.

Institutional Competency Proficiency Levels

Institutional competencies are learned and refined through education, training, and experience. By continuously developing institutional competencies as people assume greater responsibility in the organization, the Air Force is able to execute and sustain the full spectrum of airpower.

Although all Airmen execute institutional competencies, there is variation in terms of proficiency levels across ranks, positions, and grades. Airmen are educated in these competencies over the course of their careers.

An Airman's understanding of the subcompetencies varies based on where the Airman is in his or her career. Each subcompetency contains five levels of proficiency, defined below:

- ✪ **Basic** – Airmen are focused on learning and developing a foundation skill set. They face similar challenges, have limited responsibilities, and are given narrowly focused tasks.

- ✪ **Intermediate** – Airmen continue to learn and develop professional skills, understand how to leverage other professionals and knowledge sources, and begin to apply knowledge of the assigned objectives to their work.

- ✪ **Proficient** – Airmen leverage knowledge of issues and objectives to design and develop solutions. They understand how actions taken in one area of competence impact other related areas, and establish and manage the scope and quality of those areas of an assignment for which they are responsible. They may manage complex organizations.

- ✪ **Skilled** – Airmen leverage knowledge of strategies and issues to develop, present, and implement solutions. They consult with other subject matter experts and have a deep understanding how actions taken in one area of competence impact other related areas within proposed solutions. They contribute to the development of new levels of capabilities by articulating the added value of proposed solutions to leadership and staff and are considered subject matter experts within their organizational area. In addition, they may manage large, complex multi-tiered organizations.

✪ **Advanced** – Airmen impact the organization and the Air Force by leveraging their knowledge and expertise across the theater to identify and address the critical success factors for complex areas. They apply knowledge of the strategic alignment of solutions with Air Force mission objectives and serve as recognized subject matter experts inside and outside their own organizations and represent the Air Force to external organizations. In addition, they may manage large, complex multi-tiered organizations.

Subcompetency: Global, Regional, and Cultural Awareness				
Basic	**Intermediate**	**Proficient**	**Skilled**	**Advanced**
Identifies the factors influencing defense, domestic, and foreign policy; seeks to understand cultural and language norms/customs. Recognizes differences in culture, globally and regionally, and recognizes the broad impact of global culture on defense, domestic, and foreign policy.	Predicts how factors such as history, politics, availability of resources (financial, informational, technological, material, energy, warfare, and human) and economic environment of cultures that are relevant to one's mission, the USAF, and US government policy could impact mission success. Develops linguistic skills while absorbing cultural commonalities.	Applies knowledge and skills when meeting cultural challenges; maintains focus on success and on effectively handling cross-cultural challenges.	Integrates information from multiple sources to develop a well-formed yet flexible view of international issues that can be used as a basis for decision-making and relationship building.	Evaluates and synthesizes multi-cultural understanding, global economic, political and social awareness to identify opportunities and threats when formulating strategy and evaluating impact of mission implementation.

Figure 3.2. Sample of Descriptive Behavior Proficiency Levels

Each subcompetency has descriptive behaviors that dictate the performance action that must be exhibited for its five proficiency levels. Due to education, training, and experience, as Airmen progress through their careers, their understanding of the subcompetency grows and their behaviors shift from "Basic" toward "Advanced."[51] Figure 3.2 provides an example of the descriptive behaviors in the proficiency levels for the subcompetency of Global, Regional, and Cultural Awareness.

---

[51] For a complete list of descriptive behaviors at the different proficiency levels, see AFI 36-2641, *Force Development Execution*.

Measurement of education, training, and experience is a critical part of the force development process. Therefore, competency assessment should lead to more effective management of performance, which encompasses the force development process.

The competency assessment initiative should provide feedback on how well the Institutional Competency Developmental Programs' (military education and training schools/institutions) curricula and course content are aligned with the institutional competencies and how well the programs are helping students to perform the prescribed enterprise competencies. Some of the benefits of assessing the institutional competencies are:

- ✪ Ensuring institutional competencies are delivered as designed by the descriptive behaviors at the appropriate proficiency levels.

- ✪ Identifying gaps that could exist in the execution of the institutional competencies allowing opportunity for improvement.

- ✪ Improving outcome results of the institutional competency process.

Institutional competencies are used to develop and assess Airmen for the needs of the Air Force. They assist in communicating desired behaviors at the appropriate performance level, control costs, and increase productivity. Assessing the institutional competencies is a critical component of the force development construct employed by the Air Force.

COMMON GUIDING PRINCIPLES

Certain common principles guide education, training, and experience for force development at the tactical, operational, and strategic levels:

- ✪ **Build skill set expertise**. Design education and training programs with the experience and current skill levels of the participants in mind. *Tactical-level* education and training should take into account the relative inexperience and developing knowledge level of young Airmen. Programs for junior Airmen, both officer and enlisted, should focus on individual tasks that gradually increase in complexity and realism. *Operational-level* programs should leverage the skills already developed to broaden the Airmen's perspectives and capabilities, and offer them formal and informal leadership opportunities to enhance their growth. *Strategic* education and training should shift away from functional expertise and look more at leadership and assessment skills, joint and coalition integration, and policy formulation. Every training program should have established performance or competency requirements to measure success in building the required skill sets. It is necessary to maintain a balance between academic concepts, operational reality, and lessons of the past.

President Kennedy with Generals Curtis LeMay and Thomas Power

...The Air Force officer of today and tomorrow requires...scholarship. He requires breadth of learning and outlook which was rarely required in earlier days.... We need men who can cope with the challenge of new political situations as well as new enemy weapons—who can keep their forces flexible as well as reliable....

—President John F. Kennedy

○ **Prepare for change.** Skills development should keep pace with changing operational environments and resulting changing requirements. Educators should survey training methods outside of organizational bounds (other Services, government, and industry) to stay abreast of new training and education insights and best practices and adapt these methods to the programs for training and educating the force. They should review current doctrine to provide their lessons with the currency that the most recently identified best practices can provide. They should ensure educational programs are relevant using operational feedback mechanisms such as lessons learned, hot-wash sessions, after-action reports, intelligence summaries, and similar current operations tools.

○ **Create depth of expertise.** Competence and credibility require depth of experience that provides a foundation for effective leadership. Depth is not gained overnight, but is honed over time. Programs designed to develop leaders should provide the fundamentals that are reinforced by on-the-job training and expeditionary field experience. Challenging duty opportunities normally prove more effective in developing depth of expertise. *Tactical-level* education and training should concentrate on building depth of knowledge and experience in the primary skill and skill-related areas, including an understanding of Air Force culture and values. *Operational-level* education and training should build on early skills and deepen an Airman's understanding of the complete Air Force employment capability and its interface with joint and coalition partners. At the *strategic level*, education and training polish the leadership of all Airmen and command skills of officers, deepening their joint and coalition warfare and policy-making skills.

○ **Train to mission demands.** Training that meets mission needs leverages both training resources and duty experience to maximum effect. Skill expertise should prepare individuals for all tasks they are expected to perform to meet mission demands, and these needs may change rapidly with policy or international events. Mission needs may require functional specialists to train in other areas, including augmenting other Services. Educators and trainers should study the current and perceived future requirements of the operational and warfighting community and craft programs to meet those requirements.

- ○ **Train like we fight.** Success hinges on practicing the profession of arms in the same manner it will be executed on the battlefield or during a contingency. Doctrine gives trainers a clear starting point for creating programs that reflect the realities of today's operating environment. Training programs should be aligned with expected outcomes and provide realistic experience to greatly improve skill competency. Stress, unpredictability, fatigue, night operations, adverse weather, simulated equipment breakdowns, and chemical and biological contamination are examples of the challenges our Airmen will face in the field and should be trained to overcome. If training or exercises do not reflect the stress and challenges of actual conditions, then our Airmen will not be prepared when called upon to execute their mission.

- ○ **Make training and education available.** In today's high-tempo world, the opportunities to train or receive education have become more challenging. Education and training should be responsive to this shift. Commanders and supervisors should ensure they provide their people the training or education they need to meet mission requirements and for their own advancement. Educators and trainers should continue to expand the opportunities for training through online or other reachback capabilities. Education and training programs may become shorter or more flexible and adaptive to ensure coverage of the material in an expeditionary environment. Education and training may be more challenging to get while deployed, but should not be neglected for that reason.

- ○ **Validate education and training through wargames and exercises.** Simulation through exercises and wargames can be very effective in terms of time, cost, and experience gained toward preparing Airmen for their wartime and contingency roles. Exercises and wargames are effective methods of building individual experience under controlled conditions. In addition to providing instruction, these also aid in evaluating performance and the effectiveness of other training and education programs. Exercises contribute to training objectives, while wargaming is typically more appropriate for education in which critical thinking objectives are important. Exercises are also important tools in developing individual skill sets along with organizational capabilities. For example, the ULCHI FREEDOM

By embracing the training of future generations as a key principle of leadership, we ensure our successors are trained by professionals who pass on their knowledge and experience.

—General John P. Jumper, CSAF, 2001-2005

GUARDIAN exercise provides an opportunity for commanders and staffs to focus on operational and strategic issues associated with general military operations on the Korean peninsula. Wargames offer additional tools for developing and evaluating competencies of individuals and organizations.

While education and training are the foundations for an Airman's development, experience is gained when Airmen apply what they have learned to the Air Force's missions and tasks. The Air Force lessons learned process provides a ready tool for Airmen to obtain insights into the experiences of others, avoiding the difficulty of having to relearn pre-existing elements of knowledge hard-won by others.[52]

---

[52] Air Force lessons learned are available on the Air Force's joint lessons learned information system website: https://www.jllis.mil/USAF/

CONCLUSION

Leadership is fundamental to the US Air Force. Creating future Air Force leaders is the responsibility of the current leaders, and force development is their tool to do so. By using the organized approach of developing leaders from the tactical expertise level, through operational competence, leading to the most senior strategic vision levels in the Air Force, the Service will ensure its continued preeminent position in the world. The Airman's perspective and core values provide the foundation for developing and nurturing the Airmen of today and tomorrow. Through the force development framework, the Air Force will educate, train, and provide the experiences necessary to grow our future Airmen and develop the leadership attributes required to meet the challenges of a constantly changing and extremely complex international security environment. Leaders are inextricably linked to mission effectiveness; developing Airmen with a deliberate process enables the Air Force to produce the requisite leaders. **Leadership and force development will continue to provide the Air Force with its most valuable asset: its motivated and superbly qualified Airmen.**

If we should have to fight, we should be prepared to do so from the neck up instead of from the neck down.

—General James H. Doolittle

General Doolittle leading the 18 April 1942 raid on Tokyo.

AT THE VERY HEART OF WARFARE LIES DOCTRINE.....

REFERENCES

Air Force Doctrine Documents

All Air Force personnel should be familiar with the full breadth of Air Force operations. As a beginning, they should read the entire series of the capstone and keystone operational doctrine documents. All AFDDs are available on the LeMay Center for Doctrine Development and Education's website:
https://wwwmil.maxwell.af.mil/au/lemay/main.asp, the Air Force electronic publications page: https://www.e-publishing.af.mil,
or the LeMay Center for Doctrine's Community of Practice website:
https://afkm.wpafb.af.mil/community/views/home.aspx?Filter=OO-OP-AF-44.

The Community of Practice website also contains numerous additional suggested readings on leadership.

Chief of Staff of the Air Force Reading List

The Chief of Staff of the Air Force Reading List is available for review at:
http://www.af.mil/library/csafreading/index.asp

APPENDIX A

THE OATHS OF OFFICE AND ENLISTMENT

Oath of Office	Oath of Enlistment
I (FULL NAME),	I (FULL NAME),
HAVING BEEN APPOINTED A (Grade in which appointed) IN THE UNITED STATES AIR FORCE,	(NOTE: Text at left is for commissioned officers only)
DO SOLEMNLY SWEAR (OR AFFIRM)	DO SOLEMNLY SWEAR (OR AFFIRM)
THAT I WILL SUPPORT AND DEFEND THE CONSTITUTION OF THE UNITED STATES AGAINST ALL ENEMIES FOREIGN AND DOMESTIC,	THAT I WILL SUPPORT AND DEFEND THE CONSTITUTION OF THE UNITED STATES AGAINST ALL ENEMIES FOREIGN AND DOMESTIC,
THAT I WILL BEAR TRUE FAITH AND ALLEGIANCE TO THE SAME,	THAT I WILL BEAR TRUE FAITH AND ALLEGIANCE TO THE SAME,
THAT I TAKE THIS OBLIGATION FREELY WITHOUT ANY MENTAL RESERVATION OR PURPOSE OF EVASION	
AND THAT I WILL WELL AND FAITHFULLY DISCHARGE THE DUTIES OF THE OFFICE UPON WHICH I AM ABOUT TO ENTER,	AND THAT I WILL OBEY THE ORDERS OF THE PRESIDENT OF THE UNITED STATES AND THE ORDERS OF THE OFFICERS APPOINTED OVER ME ACCORDING TO REGULATIONS AND THE UNIFORM CODE OF MILITARY JUSTICE,
SO HELP ME GOD.	SO HELP ME GOD.

Why we administer an oath of office or enlistment:

○ **Legal Requirements.** Federal law (5 U.S.C. §3331 for the oath of office used for officers and civilians; 10 U.S.C. §502 for the oath of enlistment) requires persons enlisting in the Armed Forces, or persons elected or appointed to a position of honor or profit in the government of the United States, to subscribe to an oath before beginning in the position. Any individual enlisting in, or elected or appointed to an office of honor or profit in the civil service or uniformed Services, takes the appropriate oath, as shown above.

✪ **Ethical Purpose.** By executing the oath of office/enlistment when they accept the commission or appointment, Airmen make a promise—an ethical agreement or bond of a person's word.

It is with these oaths that Airmen first commit to the basic core values, placing service to the Constitution before self. It is where we place integrity on the line by giving our word as our bond. It is where we swear (or affirm) to "well and faithfully" discharge our duties, or obey orders to do so, thus committing ourselves to excellence. The oaths are distinct in that the allegiance established is to the ideals of the Constitution, not to any individual or organization. This source for the oaths gives them their greatest strength.

APPENDIX B

CODE OF CONDUCT FOR MEMBERS OF THE ARMED FORCES OF THE UNITED STATES

Executive Order 10631--Code of Conduct for members of the Armed Forces of the United States[53]

Source: The provisions of Executive Order 10631 of Aug. 17, 1955, appear at 20 FR 6057, 3 CFR, 1954-1958 Comp., p. 266, unless otherwise noted.

By virtue of the authority vested in me as President of the United States, and as Commander in Chief of the armed forces of the United States, I hereby prescribe the Code of Conduct for Members of the Armed Forces of the United States which is attached to this order and hereby made a part thereof.

All members of the Armed Forces of the United States are expected to measure up to the standards embodied in this Code of Conduct while in combat or in captivity. To ensure achievement of these standards, members of the armed forces liable to capture shall be provided with specific training and instruction designed to better equip them to counter and withstand all enemy efforts against them, and shall be fully instructed as to the behavior and obligations expected of them during combat or captivity.

[Second paragraph amended by EO 12633 of Mar. 28, 1988, 53 FR 10355, 3 CFR, 1988 Comp., p. 561]

The Secretary of Defense (and the Secretary of Transportation with respect to the Coast Guard except when it is serving as part of the Navy[54]) shall take such action as is deemed necessary to implement this order and to disseminate and make the said Code known to all members of the armed forces of the United States.

[Third paragraph amended by EO 11382 of Nov. 28, 1967, 32 FR 16247, 3 CFR, 1966-1970 Comp., p. 691]

Code of Conduct for Members of the United States Armed Forces

I

I am an American, fighting in the forces which guard my country and our way of life. I am prepared to give my life in their defense.

---

[53] As published in the Federal Register: http://www.archives.gov/federal-register/codification/executive-order/10631.html, accessed 10 March 2009.

[54] Since the promulgation of this executive order, the Coast Guard has been transferred to the Department of Homeland Security.

[Article I amended by EO 12633 of Mar. 28, 1988, 53 FR 10355, 3 CFR, 1988 Comp., p. 561]

II

I will never surrender of my own free will. If in command, I will never surrender the members of my command while they still have the means to resist.

[Article II amended by EO 12633 of Mar. 28, 1988, 53 FR 10355, 3 CFR, 1988 Comp., p. 561]

III

If I am captured I will continue to resist by all means available. I will make every effort to escape and aid others to escape. I will accept neither parole nor special favors from the enemy.

IV

If I become a prisoner of war, I will keep faith with my fellow prisoners. I will give no information or take part in any action which might be harmful to my comrades. If I am senior, I will take command. If not, I will obey the lawful orders of those appointed over me and will back them up in every way.

V

When questioned, should I become a prisoner of war, I am required to give name, rank, service number and date of birth. I will evade answering further questions to the utmost of my ability. I will make no oral or written statements disloyal to my country and its allies or harmful to their cause.

[Article V amended by EO 12017 of Nov. 3, 1977, 42 FR 57941, 3 CFR, 1977 Comp., p. 152]

VI

I will never forget that I am an American, fighting for freedom, responsible for my actions, and dedicated to the principles which made my country free. I will trust in my God and in the United States of America.

[Article VI amended by EO 12633 of Mar. 28, 1988, 53 FR 10355, 3 CFR, 1988 Comp., p. 561]

APPENDIX C

INSTITUTIONAL COMPETENCY LIST

Category	Competency	Subcompetency
Personal	Embodies Airman Culture	- Ethical Leadership - Followership - Warrior Ethos - Develops Self
	Communicating	- Speaking and Writing - Active Listening
People/Team	Leading People	- Develops and Inspires Others - Takes Care of People - Diversity
	Fostering Collaborative Relationships	- Builds Teams and Coalitions - Negotiating
Organizational	Employing Military Capabilities	- Operational and Strategic Art - Unit, Air Force, Joint, and Coalition Capabilities - Non-adversarial Crisis Response
	Enterprise Perspective	- Enterprise Structure and Relationships - Government Organization and Processes - Global, Regional, and Cultural Awareness - Strategic Communication
	Managing Organizations and Resources	- Resource Stewardship - Change Management - Continuous Improvement
	Strategic Thinking	- Vision - Decision-making - Adaptability

PERSONAL COMPETENCIES

Personal competencies are those institutional competencies leaders need in face-to-face and interpersonal relationships that directly influence human behavior and values. These are foundational institutional competencies learned at the tactical level that will continue to play a critical role as leaders move to the operational competence and strategic vision levels. Personal competencies are essential for individual contribution, for building cohesive units and for empowering immediate subordinates. Each competency below is followed by the relevant subcompetencies that define it.

Embodies Airman Culture

✪ **Ethical Leadership**

   ✪ ✪ Promotes Air Force core values (integrity first, service before self, excellence in all we do) through goals, actions, and referent behaviors.

   ✪ ✪ Develops trust and commitment through words and actions.

   ✪ ✪ Accountable for areas of responsibility, operations of unit, and personal actions.

   ✪ ✪ Maintains checks and balances on self and others.

✪ **Followership**

   ✪ ✪ Comprehends and values the essential role of followership in mission accomplishment.

   ✪ ✪ Seeks command, guidance, and/or leadership while providing unbiased advice.

   ✪ ✪ Aligns priorities and actions toward chain of command guidance for mission accomplishment.

   ✪ ✪ Exercises flexibility and adapts quickly to alternating role as leader/follower: follower first, leader at times.

✪ **Warrior Ethos**

   ✪ ✪ Exhibits a hardiness of spirit despite physical and mental hardships—moral and physical courage.

   ✪ ✪ Continuously hones their skills to support the employment of military capabilities.

   ✪ ✪ Displays military/executive bearing, self-discipline, and self control.

✪ **Develops Self**

   ✪ ✪ Assesses self to identify strengths and developmental needs.

   ✪ ✪ Seeks and incorporates feedback on own performance; aware of personal impact on others.

✪ ✪ Continually increases breadth and depth of knowledge and skills; develops life-long learning habits.

Communicating

✪ Speaking and Writing

✪ ✪ Articulates ideas and intent in a clear, concise, and convincing manner through both verbal and written communication.

✪ ✪ Adjusts communication approach to unique operational environment and audience needs.

✪ ✪ Effectively creates communication bridges among units, organizations and institutions.

✪ Active Listening

✪ ✪ Fosters the free flow of ideas in an atmosphere of open exchange.

✪ ✪ Actively attempts to understand others' points of view and clarifies information as needed.

✪ ✪ Solicits feedback to ensure that others understand messages as they were intended.

PEOPLE/TEAM COMPETENCIES

This group of competencies involves more interpersonal and team relationships. They represent competencies that, when combined with the personal competencies, are essential as leaders move on to lead larger groups or organizations. People/team leadership competencies are usually exercised more indirectly than personal leadership competencies. Leaders use these competencies to set the organizational climate. Each competency below is followed by the relevant subcompetencies that define it.

Leading People

✪ Develops and Inspires Others

✪ ✪ Helps and motivates others to improve their skills and enhance their performance through feedback, coaching, mentoring, and delegating.

✪ ✪ Empowers others and guides them in the direction of their goals and mission accomplishment.

✪ ✪ Inspires others to transcend their own self-interests and embrace personal sacrifice and risk for the good of the organization and mission.

✪ Takes Care of People

- ✪ ✪ People first—attends to the physical, mental, ethical, and spiritual well-being of fellow Airmen and their families.

- ✪ ✪ Creates an environment where Airmen take care of Airmen 24/7, 365 days a year, including leaders, peers, and subordinates; integrates wellness into mission accomplishment.

- ✪ ✪ Establishes work-life balance through time management and setting clear expectations and priorities.

✪ Diversity

- ✪ ✪ Leverages differences in individual characteristics, experiences, and abilities.

- ✪ ✪ Leverages diversity for mission accomplishment and fosters an inclusive environment.

- ✪ ✪ Shows respect for others regardless of the situation; treats people in an equitable manner.

Fostering Collaborative Relationships

✪ Builds Teams and Coalitions

- ✪ ✪ Builds effective teams for goal and mission accomplishment and improves team performance.

- ✪ ✪ Contributes to group identity while fostering cohesiveness, confidence, and cooperation.

- ✪ ✪ Sees and attends to the interests, goals, and values of other individuals and institutions.

- ✪ ✪ Develops networks and alliances that span organizational, Service, department, agency, and national boundaries.

✪ Negotiating

- ✪ ✪ Understands the underlying principles and concepts applied before, during, and after a negotiation.

- ✪ ✪ Attains desired mission outcomes while maintaining positive, long-term relationships with key individuals and groups.

- ✪ ✪ Uses appropriate interpersonal styles and methods to reduce tension or conflict between two or more people, anticipates and addresses conflict constructively, and anticipates and prevents counter-productive confrontations.

✪ ✪ Persuades and influences others; builds consensus; gains cooperation; effectively collaborates.

ORGANIZATIONAL COMPETENCIES

These competencies represent those applicable at all levels of the Air Force but are most in demand at the strategic level. Strategic leaders apply organizational competencies to establish structure and articulate strategic vision. Effective organizational competency skills include technical competence on force structure and integration; on unified, joint, multinational, and interagency operations; on resource allocation; and on management of complex systems. In addition, they apply to conceptual competence in creating policy and vision and interpersonal skills emphasizing consensus building and influencing peers and other policy makers, both internal and external to the organization. This level is the nexus of warfighting leadership skills for the Air Force. It is achieved through having learned the lessons from the other types of institutional competencies (i.e., personal and people/team). Each competency below is followed by the relevant subcompetencies that define it.

Employing Military Capabilities

✪ **Operational and Strategic Art**

✪ ✪ Understands and applies operational and strategic art in conventional and irregular warfare, peacekeeping, and homeland operations.

✪ ✪ Demonstrates expertise in integrating and leveraging doctrine, concepts, and capabilities within an effects-based approach to operations.

✪ ✪ Uses innovation and technology in the employment of lethal and nonlethal force.

✪ **Unit, Air Force, Joint, and Coalition Capabilities**

✪ ✪ Considers and applies capabilities of the Air Force across air, space, and cyberspace.

✪ ✪ Understands how Air Force capabilities relate and complement other Service capabilities.

✪ ✪ Understands interdependencies and interoperability across Services, agencies, departments, and coalition partners.

✪ **Non-adversarial Crisis Response**

✪ ✪ Recognizes the national security implications of peacekeeping operations, humanitarian relief operations, and support to civil authorities, both foreign and domestic.

✪ ✪ Understands the need for engagement before and after warfighting or crisis response, the need for integrated involvement with interagency and multinational partners, and the need for multipurpose capabilities that can be applied across the range of military operations.

Enterprise Perspective

✪ Enterprise Structure and Relationships

✪ ✪ Understands the organizational structure and relationships between the Air Force, the Department of Defense (DOD), the joint staff, the combatant commands, the defense agencies, and other elements of the defense structure.

✪ ✪ Understands how one's function or unit fits into its parent organizations.

✪ ✪ Understands how one's parent organization relates to its external environment—supporting and supported organizations, the public, Congress, etc.

✪ Government Organization and Processes

✪ ✪ Understands essential operating features and functions of the Air Force, DOD, the national security structure, other related executive branch functions, and Congress, to include leadership and organization; roles of members, committees, and staffs; authorization, appropriation, and budget processes; acquisition policy and procedures; and interdependencies and relationships.

✪ Global, Regional, and Cultural Awareness

✪ ✪ Conscious of regional and other factors influencing defense, domestic, and foreign policy.

✪ ✪ Seeks to understand foreign cultural, religious, political, organizational, and societal norms and customs.

✪ ✪ Develops linguistic skills.

✪ Strategic Communication

✪ ✪ Informs and appropriately influences key audiences by synchronizing and integrating communication efforts to deliver truthful, timely, accurate, and credible information, analysis, and opinion.

✪ ✪ Formulates the institutional message, telling the Air Force story.

Managing Organizations and Resources

✪ Resource Stewardship

✪ ✪ Identifies, acquires, administers, and conserves financial, informational, technological, material, warfare, and human resources needed to accomplish the mission.

✪ ✪ Implements "best practice" management techniques throughout the organization.

✪ Change Management

✪ ✪ Embraces, supports, and leads change.

✪ ✪ Understands the change management process, critical success factors, and common problems and costs.

✪ ✪ Perceives opportunities and risks before or as they emerge.

✪ Continuous Improvement

✪ ✪ Originates action to improve existing conditions and processes, using appropriate methods to identify opportunities, implement solutions, and measure impact.

✪ ✪ Supports ongoing commitment to improve processes, products, services, and people.

✪ ✪ Anticipates and meets the needs of both internal and external stakeholders.

Strategic Thinking

✪ Vision

✪ ✪ Takes a long-term view and builds a shared vision that clearly defines and expresses a future state.

✪ ✪ Provides innovative and creative insights and solutions for guiding and directing organizations to meet institutional needs.

✪ ✪ Formulates effective plans and strategies for consistently achieving goals and maximizing mission accomplishment.

✪ ✪ Anticipates potential threats, barriers, and opportunities; encourages risk-taking.

✪ Decision-making

✪ ✪ Identifies, evaluates, and assimilates data and information from multiple streams and differentiates information according to its utility; uses information to influence actions and decisions.

✪ ✪ Uses analytic methods in solving problems and developing alternatives.

✪ ✪ Makes sound, well-informed, and timely decisions despite conditions of ambiguity, risk, and uncertainty.

✪ ✪ Analyzes situations critically to anticipate second and third order effects of proposed policies or actions.

✪ ✪ Establishes metrics to evaluate results and adapts and implements feedback.

✪ Adaptability

✪ ✪ Maintains effectiveness when experiencing major changes in work tasks or environment.

✪ ✪ Adjusts to change within new work structures, processes, requirements, and cultures.

✪ ✪ Responds quickly and proactively to ambiguous and emerging conditions, opportunities, and risks.

As leaders move through successively higher echelons in the Air Force, they need a wider portfolio of competencies that are typically gained at previous levels of leadership. As military and civilian leaders progress within the Air Force, they serve in more complex and interdependent organizations, have increased personal responsibility and authority, and have significantly different institutional competencies than their subordinates.

APPENDIX D

EDUCATION AND TRAINING

Developing people to lead the world's best air, space, and cyberspace force takes the personal commitment of all Airmen—a commitment to focus on developing ourselves and encouraging our fellow Airmen—to learn as much as possible about the complexities of our profession of arms. I am committed to supporting you as you take on these new challenges.

—Michael W. Wynne, SECAF, 2006

Education and training facilitate the transition from one level of experience to the next and are critical to creating productive experiences in an Airman's development. Force development seeks to provide experiences that deliberately develop tactical expertise, operational competence, and strategic vision. Airmen who are prepared for the experiences to come are not only better able to perform their assigned duties, but also gain more from each experience. Skills training and developmental education are foundational to preparing the Airman for developmental experiences, and it is critical to employ the proper approach. Although interdependent, education and training are fundamentally distinct in application. Education prepares individuals for dynamic environments, while training is essential in developing skill sets. Education and training are complementary and will commonly overlap; however, recognition of the distinction between them is essential to the approach taken. Training approaches applied to educational situations will be less effective, as will educational approaches applied to situations in which training is more appropriate. The following items distinguish education from training in several critical areas:

○ **Training** is appropriate when standardized outcomes are required. Training is focused on building specific skill sets to produce reliable, consistent results. Although skill application involves judgment, it is the purpose of training to teach skills that are associated with desired outcomes. (When repairing jet engines, for example, it is desirable to have the engine meet standardized performance measures upon completion of the repair tasks—proper training ensures a standardized, predictable outcome.) Standardization in training and evaluation helps commanders to ensure outcomes are predictable. Tasks (the tangible questions to be dealt with), conditions (the operating environment where the function is to be performed), and standards (the minimum of acceptable proficiency) are vital to the training process.

○ **Education** is appropriate when adaptive outcomes are desired. Education is focused on developing critical thought that enables creative solutions. Although creative thought may involve skill application, it is the purpose of critical thought to form successful solutions to new problems. (An engineer, for example, is able to design a new jet engine that exceeds all known performance measures through application of creative design concepts and unusual materials applications.)

○ **Training** is task dependent. Training is generally focused on a specific skill. Although specialties may be quite complex, each is composed of elements having distinct tasks that when correctly performed lead to successful, predictable outcomes. (When operating a radar system, for example, power-up is distinct from data recall operations and each task is required, but each task is distinct in the steps taken—proper training ensures the proper steps are followed in the proper sequence to successfully operate the system.)

○ **Education** is process dependent. Education is generally focused on combining familiar and unfamiliar information to produce a suggested course of action. The intellectual demands of consolidating past experiences and ideas with new experiences and unfamiliar information to produce new ideas depend on the process of critical thought. (Radar data, for example, only becomes useful when analyzed and screened to produce relevant information—the intellect required to make sense of multiple items forms the process of critical thought.)

○ **Training** is technically specific, focusing on specific situations and the tools of that specialty. Training is intended to develop skill sets that are generally associated with specific duty requirements. While some skill sets are generally universal (such as computer skills), specialty training is specific to a particular skill set. Skill sets are generally associated with specific duty requirements and the tools of that specialty. Training is focused on specific situations and the tools of that specialty. (A tanker boom operator, for example, would not be prepared to take on the duty requirements of a pararescue Airman or vice versa—each has received training that is specific to the technical tools of his or her duties.)

○ **Education** is not dependent on a specific situation. Because education seeks to develop critical thinking skills, it attempts to prepare individuals for new experiences and new challenges. While education can readily prepare individuals for known situations, the fundamental aim is to develop individual talents to create successful outcomes in unfamiliar situations. (For example, a weatherman, using a comprehensive understanding of atmospherics, is able to predict weather patterns across regions around the globe.)

○ **Training** requires restrictive application. Because training is generally focused on a specific skill set, the skills learned are usually limited to the specialty related to that skill set. Training aims to instill certain specific skills that when applied in a systematic and predictable way produce predictable outcomes. Training is, therefore, generally restricted in application to the known circumstances related to the skill set. (A jet engine mechanic, for example, would not be well equipped to repair a piece of complex communications equipment any more than an electronics technician could be expected to repair a jet engine.)

○ **Education** requires transformative application. Knowledge and skills, such as critical thinking, that are cultivated during education are of great benefit in unfamiliar circumstances. Education provides the individual with logic skills that encourage creative thought and allows individuals to create new solutions to unfamiliar problems. In application, education is most beneficial when transitioning from the known to the unknown. (An engineering team, for example, confronted with the task of repairing an unfamiliar foreign communications network devises a successful solution using equipment that is both familiar and foreign.)

○ **Training** is most effective within defined parameters. Training develops skill sets and the talent to successfully cope with deviations from normal, within the bounds of the specialty. Training is skill specific and variations from those normally expected circumstances are also limited to that skill set. (An aircraft hydraulics specialist, for example, is trained to deal with hydraulic systems and expected problems, but would likely not be as successful in coping with an unfamiliar hydraulic system that experiences an unfamiliar failure.)

○ **Education** is most effective outside defined parameters. The essential strength of education is to prepare individuals to create successful outcomes in unfamiliar situations. The value of education is most apparent when the individual is confronted with creating solutions beyond the set of parameters in which they may normally operate. (A hydraulic specialist, for example, relying on an understanding of hydraulic principles and system functions is able to create a solution to an unfamiliar failure.)

○ **Training** is most effective in stable, expected environments. Training generally serves to impart skills necessary for success in known situations and circumstances. Circumstances that are known as normal operating environments and situations that can be anticipated may be considered as occurring within an expected environment. Training provides the skills necessary for success in stable environments. (Emergency drills and realistic exercises, for example, help develop skills to cope with anticipated scenarios under stress or in critical situations.)

- **Education** is most effective within unexpected environments. In unexpected or unanticipated situations there are no procedures or checklists to provide guidance. Skill sets generally become less applicable in scenarios that have not been seen or practiced. Education provides the tools necessary to cope with new challenges. It is in rapidly changing environments that produce unexpected problems that education can provide the mental talents to succeed. (A fire fighter, for example, when being confronted with unmanageable flames, understands the mechanics of fires to successfully egress the situation.)

- **Training** value diminishes with uncertainty. The further the situation progresses from the talents of the individual, the less effective the individual becomes in implementing a successful solution. Because training is focused on a specialized skill set, those circumstances that fall outside of the skill set produce a greater amount of uncertainty. Thus the value of skill set training is reduced in the face of uncertainty.

- **Education** value increases with uncertainty. Education provides the tools for innovation and creative thought. In circumstances of new challenges and unfamiliar situations, education can allow individuals to create solutions to reduce uncertainty and implement successful solutions. (Combat presents leaders with many opportunities to experience unfamiliar situations, but relying on historical precedents, lessons learned in wargames and exercises, and past personal experience, leaders can develop successful strategies and tactics to prevail.)

- **Training** is not inherent in education. Learning can take place in individuals having few specialized skills. Even in unstructured environments, learning can proceed successfully. Education involves the process of learning new concepts and/or developing logic talents to create new thought. There are many examples of successful artists creating great works without a formal training in the medium. It is creative talent that is among the most beneficial results of education.

- **Education** is inherent in training. Basic talents are critical to learning. Individuals, for example, should be able to read proficiently to access training materials. Individuals must also have a good grasp of vocabulary to understand training terms and concepts. Subjects such as reading, vocabulary, mathematics, and similar topics are the product of education. Training cannot take place without first having individuals who meet the qualifications to receive training. Training that exceeds the qualifications required of the participants is less effective.

- **Training** shows immediate benefits. Learned skills can be demonstrated almost immediately. It is often part of the training process that individuals demonstrate the skills acquired. Repetition of skills serves to reinforce those skills and provides a measure of training success. (A 'three-level' technician can be placed in positions of responsibility and produce successful outcomes as a result of training.) Training usually produces immediate effects by imparting new skills or developing existing skills.

○ **Education** provides long-term benefits. Skills in critical thinking are usually not demonstrated until encountering unfamiliar circumstances. Logic skills are also developed over time through formal education and experience, thus are constantly evolving and maturing. Consequently, the benefits of education are closely linked to experience and tend to grow over time. Because logic skills are not as demonstrable as technical skills, these talents are usually not as apparent in the short term.

APPENDIX E

LEADERSHIP STUDIES

The leadership studies are intended as examples of leadership and force development and are organized around the construct of tactical expertise, operational competence, and strategic vision.

LEADERSHIP STUDY FOR TACTICAL EXPERTISE:

SECURITY POLICE DEFENSE OF TAN SON NHUT AND BIEN HOA AIR BASES, JANUARY 1968

ATTACK ORDER

From: The Presidium of the National Liberation Front Central Committee
To:
- Cadres and Soldiers of the People's Liberation Armed Forces
- Compatriots

After successive victories in recent months, the situation in-country as well as in the world becomes very favorable for the liberation of our Country and People. The American aggressors are being defeated and the Puppet Government is being on the way to disintegration. Our Revolutionary Forces are grown up and become stronger than ever. The North (VN), a large rear of the South (VN), is more and more strong and is striking the American invaders with dead-blows.

Friendly Nations on [sic] over the world (including progressive American people) unanimously and positively support us.

The presidium orders all Liberation Armed Forces, Political Struggle Force, members of all Liberation Associations and other Patriotic Forces and the whole Nation to unanimously stand up in order to:

- Destroy the enemy vital force as much as possible, defeat US and Allied troops, and liquidate Puppet government troops.

- Break down all Puppet Government Administrative organizations and severely punish Vietnamese traitors and tyrants.

- Establish Revolutionary Administration and make every effort to defend it, decidedly punish and break up all enemy counterattack forces under any circumstances.

- Carry out policies in the essential line of action promulgated by the Front.

Compatriots, Cadres, and Soldiers
Move forward bravely
We will certainly win.

The Tet offensive of January, 1968, began with limited to no intelligence available to the forces defending the installations in South Vietnam near major cities. Outside Saigon, the 377th Security Police Squadron (377 SPS) on Tan Son Nhut Air Base and the 3rd Security Police Squadron (3 SPS) at Bien Hoa Air Base were in normal alert condition until 1732 on 30 January 1968, when orders came down from the commander, 7th Air Force, putting Air Force units into "Alert Condition Red," a posture providing the commander with the option for using all security police and augmentees to provide the maximum security possible over a short period of time. According to the 377 SPS combat operations after action report, "[t]he intelligence situation for the days immediately preceeding [sic] the attack remained relatively unchanged from the normal."

The descriptions below of the actions at each base vary in their styles; for Tan Son Nhut, the information is derived from the unit after-action report, demonstrating the dynamism of the action that called for leadership at the tactical level by numerous members of the Security Police squadron. For Bien Hoa, the focus is on the recollections of one member of the Security Police squadron, emphasizing the human impact leadership can have on an individual.

Tan Son Nhut Air Base

On Tan Son Nhut, only the 377 SPS and the supporting Army Task Force (TF) 35 were placed into Alert Condition Red, with the rest of the base in Condition Yellow. When Alert Condition Red was implemented, three platoons of US Army personnel (TF 35) were alerted and placed on five-minute standby status as augmentation reserve forces for the 377 SPS, under the operational control of the commander, 377 SPS.

At 0300 on 31 January 1968, the joint defense operations center (JDOC) received notification that the US Embassy in Saigon and the Saigon radio station were under attack. At 0320, the guard in Tower 16 at the east-southeast corner of the base reported observing small arms fire from off base directed at the petroleum/oil/lubrication (POL) site on the installation. Security Police were dispatched and members of the quick reaction force (QRF) and TF 35 responded to predesignated rendezvous points. Reports of small arms, grenade, and mortar fire began to increase dramatically from various points around the base.

At 0340, the Security Police at the 051 bunker on the west side of the base reported being hit by mortar or rocket fire and the rounds were landing on base. At 0344, they reported the west perimeter fence was breached near the 051 gate. The 051 bunker was manned by five personnel: Sergeants Louis Fischer, William Cyr, Charles Hebron, Roger Mills, and Alonzo Coggins. Sergeant Fischer, in charge of the personnel at the bunker, directed its defense until enemy fire killed him, along with Sergeants Cyr, Hebron, and Mills. Sergeant Coggins survived, but was severely wounded. The assault on the west side of the base, centered around the 051 bunker, was the main thrust of the attack on Tan Son Nhut.

051 Bunker, Tan Son Nhut Air Base, January 1968

At 0529, enemy troops were sighted by Tower 1 Security Police near the Alpha/Echo sector line, to the northeast of the 051 bunker. Security Police deployed to a main line of resistance (MLR) from east to west to act as a blocking force, as the enemy had penetrated approximately 600 meters into the base in an area approximately 300 meters wide. Intense defensive resistance by the Security Police, along with TF 35 personnel and forces of the Army of the Republic of Vietnam (ARVN). stopped the attack, and by 0603, some enemy forces were observed withdrawing through a break in the perimeter fence south of the 051 gate.

At 0630, The US Army's C Troop, 3rd Squadron, 4th Cavalry, from Cu Chi arrived in the area after fighting its way down the highway to the base. This counterattack by friendly forces outside the base allowed the defenders on Tan Son Nhut to mount their own counterattack, which began at 0635.

Small arms fire continued around the perimeter of the base until 0730, with posts in the north, east, and south sectors reporting small arms and automatic weapons fire. At 0725, the defensive lines on base received heavy concentrations of fire to cover an attempted enemy assault on the friendly counterattack line. This enemy fire was used chiefly to cover the withdrawal of their wounded and the part of the main force still inside the perimeter. Fighting continued around the base for several more hours. Several attempts to recapture the 051 gate during this time were unsuccessful, but at 1210, 377 SPS personnel assaulted again and neutralized the enemy fire from there, recapturing the bunker. This was the last area of the base held by the enemy. At 1217, the base perimeter was resecured. Hostile fire continued from off base for several hours afterwards.

Bien Hoa Air Base

Simultaneous with the attack on Tan Son Nhut, North Vietnamese and Viet Cong forces totaling four battalions hit Bien Hoa Air Base, northeast of Saigon. At the time, it was the busiest air base in the world, with 150 aircraft assigned and numerous transient aircraft flowing through. When the attack occurred, the key thrust of the enemy assault centered on the east side of the base around a heavy bunker built originally by the French, named Bunker Hill 10 by the 3 SPS. The following transcription of an interview with Senior Master Sergeant (SMSgt) (Retired) William "Pete" Piazza provides a clear view of the intensity of the fighting at the time. For his actions at Bunker Hill 10, Sergeant Piazza was awarded the Silver Star. During the battle, as a staff sergeant, he was in charge of an ammunition resupply team, and had been dispatched to Bunker Hill 10 to resupply the squadron operations officer, Captain Reginald Maisey, at the bunker where he and 30 other personnel were engaged in a firefight.

Bunker Hill 10, Bien Hoa Air Base, January 1968

"We brought slap flares to Captain Maisey. He had already gone through two boxes of them; if you've ever seen elephant grass, you can hardly see anything in it. At 0330, the first RPG [rocket-propelled grenade] round hit. We were all behind the bunker at the time. There was a QRT [quick reaction team], a SAT [security alert team], even the fire department was there.

"The first RPG round hit. The M-60 gun was sitting on top of the bunker. When it got hit the M-60 fell over the edge; it was just sitting on the sandbags. We all turned around and looked at each other, and somebody said, 'Look!' and pointed up.   If you've ever seen the movie Superman, all we saw was a B-40 round coming right over the top of the bunker into the elephant grass [with sparks flying out looking like a cape].   It never went off; it was a dud.   Everybody just looked at each other, then somebody said, 'Hit the dirt,' then a 'Boom!'

"The next round hit the bunker and that's when the fire department personnel decided to get the hell out of there.   Captain Maisey had the 145th Aviation Battalion coordinator that was supposed to be in CSC (central security control) if we needed him because we didn't have communication radios with them.   We'd call CSC who in turn would call 145th aviation headquarters and then the choppers would go.   Well, the coordinator was out at Bunker Hill 10 with us, so we had no way of talking with the Army.   He was sitting behind the bunker with an M-16 with the XM-148 grenade launcher (which evolved into the M-203 rifle with grenade launcher), sitting there not knowing what to do with it; he's a pilot, not a rifleman.   I gave him my CAR-15 [rifle] and I took the XM-148 with the M-16 attached, and took the rounds he had.

"I could see Charlie because I was on the right-hand side of the bunker.   I could see the firing coming at us.   There were two posts out in front of that, both were Quan Canh [Vietnamese Air Force security police] posts…. That was our first information that Charlie was coming because the guys that got out alive ran down to Bunker Hill 10 in their underwear screaming, 'VC, VC, VC!'

"We got into a situation like, when you're sitting in a theater watching a western, one guy comes out and fires from behind a building, the other guy waits till the round hits, then comes out and shoots, then ducks back behind the building.   Charlie fired 13 RPGs at us, and I fired 9 or 10 rounds.   My last round hit 'em, because there was a big explosion, and all I saw were three bodies and a big flash.   I must have hit whatever ammunition they had with 'em.   It was a lucky shot.

"Before they blew, they fired a shot that hit here [pointing to a photo of the bunker, low firing point slit]; I figured that was the one that killed Captain Maisey.   He was inside, talking on the radio, and the 13th round, because I got 'em on the next round, burrowed through the bunker and caught him square in the back.   Unfortunately, there wasn't enough light inside; we knew somebody had been hit and killed, but didn't know who.

"When the 145th Aviation Battalion started firing with miniguns from gunships and such, I decided to get the hell out of Dodge and went inside the bunker.   I tripped over the person.   We picked him up and carried him outside, but we still did not know it was Captain Maisey at the time.   Matter of fact, we didn't know it was him until the sun came up.   [For his efforts defending Bien Hoa Air Base from the North Vietnamese attack during Tet on 30-31 January 1968, Captain Maisey was awarded the Air Force Cross posthumously.]

"I was about 24-25 years old, not the youngest guy, not the oldest guy out there. One of the things that really kept everybody together was this lieutenant colonel here (gesturing to Lt Col Kent Miller, 3 SPS commander, seated next to him) got on the radio and he started talking to us like he was right with us, and he started telling us, 'Understand, calm down, calm down; you know what you gotta do; tell me what's going on,' in a calm voice. It really calmed everybody down. One of the guys told me a couple of hours later when the colonel came in and told 'em 'you guys do what you gotta do, I'll be on the radio and be the communicator to make sure everybody knows what's going on. You take care of the basics and let me do this;' he took over the radio and he just started talking to us. I say the old man calmed us down, and he did. That really was a plus factor. A lot of officers you hear about, 'I'm going to lead you in the charge,' well, he led us in a way that a lot of people would not think of, and today I know several officers that follow in this gentleman's footsteps, in that they don't try to get out in front like Custer and yell charge. Take your time, move along cautiously, you know what's going on, what you've got to do, so do your job."

Leadership in the Security Police during Tet, 31 January 1968[55]

These very abbreviated descriptions of operations during the battles for Tan Son Nhut and Bien Hoa are necessary for full comprehension of what occurred, but are only part of what is needed to understand why the US forces were victorious. The leadership, specifically the tactical leadership by the officers, noncommissioned officers, and Airmen of the 377 and 3 SPS, proved to be the key to their success. Leaders at all levels overcame inhibiting factors to accomplish their mission.

A common theme among veterans of this set of actions was the frustration with the lack of training and equipment to accomplish the duties they were tasked to perform. There was a continuing challenge for the unit leadership to obtain the requisite equipment they believed was necessary to perform their tasks. At Tan Son Nhut, the Airmen on the MLR had chronic shortness of ammunition: "We had a severe problem with ammo resupply," stated one member who felt the lack of ammunition on his post. At Bien Hoa, the resupply system established by the commander, Lt Col Kent Miller, and executed at the NCO level, was robust, but the equipment limitations hampered its effectiveness even so: "During the battle, some of the troops still ran out of ammunition because of a lack of magazines. The rounds were handed out, and they had to fill their magazines. You got bandoliers and had to strip them into the magazines yourself."

As is common with many organizations, one of the most vexing problems dealt with by the unit leadership was insufficient and ineffective communication. At Tan Son Nhut, "There were big gaps in communications...the Army ran JDOC...the tower called in forces [observed at the base perimeter], that was relayed to CSC, then to JDOC, and

---

[55] Quotations throughout are from first-person interviews with veterans of the battles at Tan Son Nhut and Bien Hoa. They volunteered their memories over the course of five days during a reunion of the Vietnam Security Police Association (http://www.vspa.com/), October, 2006. The author is indebted to them for their forthrightness and openness in discussing leadership as they observed it at that time and place.

we got the word it was friendly forces…Those 'friendly forces' were actually NVA [North Vietnamese Army] battalions." For one Airman posted in an internal patrol on the base, information that an attack had commenced came abruptly: "The only thing that alerted me to the attack was the helicopter gunships going over my head, shooting those miniguns, and the casings were hitting my helmet." At Bien Hoa, the squadron commander, having been in the position for 11 ½ months before the battle, continued to be rankled by the lack of accurate and actionable intelligence coming from organizations tasked to provide that information. In describing the value of intelligence from 7th Air Force and Military Assistance Command-Vietnam (MACV), it was "nonexistent; nonreliable [sic] anyway."

In contrast, all members interviewed expressed praise for the leadership within their units, reserving the highest accolades for the officers and noncommissioned officers who demonstrated competence during the battle: "We were not trained properly, we did not have the right equipment, intelligence was horrible, but we had some wonderful officers and NCOs who kept it together." "The NCO leadership really kept you alive. You weren't prepared for what happened, you were in shock. The NCOs led us through that."

"Some people didn't get recognized for leadership until something happens and their leadership comes out…It's not always recognized." In positions of command and control, both officers and NCOs presented the strongest front of guidance and direction for the forces in contact with the enemy. At Tan Son Nhut, the NCOIC in CSC, Technical Sergeant (TSgt) James Bloom, provided a voice of calm and efficiency readily recognized by the forces on the line: "If it were not for him…he was the key…he knew what he was doing." On one occasion, he forcibly removed an officer from CSC who was impeding his efforts to obtain accurate information from the field. The 377 SPS operations officer, Major Carl Bender, was not known for his approachability on a daily basis, "Nobody liked him because he had no personality," but during the attack, he proved to be a rock of competence to the troops: "He was the most incredible officer…." He was severely wounded during the battle, driving himself to the aid station, stopping his jeep by running it into a pole, then directing the personnel how to put him into a stretcher.

At Bien Hoa, the 3 SPS personnel reserved their highest praise for Lt Col Kent Miller, the squadron commander. His leadership during the battle was seen as steady, calming, and, appropriately, commanding. By his own admission, he actually made only "about six orders during the whole battle." He stated one of his biggest contributions was to decide on the call signs "Big Ears 1 and 2" for listening posts. In reality, his leadership was felt long before 0320, 31 Jan 68, as expressed by Sergeant Piazza: "The thing that set apart the officers we had, from the colonel to Captain Maisey, the operations officer, [and the other officers in the squadron], was that, in their hearts and minds, if you're going to do something for the troops you have to train them."

Lt Col Miller initiated a training program for his forces, known as Eagle Flight, in an effort to provide his personnel combat training. This effort was a conscious decision to improve the survivability of Security Police even though it had to circumvent the directive that Security Police were restricted to actions inside the base perimeter, with the Army maintaining the responsibility to secure the perimeter outside the wire. He obtained training from the 173rd Airborne Brigade, US Army, who were located in a base camp to the east of Bien Hoa. His all-volunteer force received intensive air assault training, culminating in their establishing a circular defense at a landing zone several kilometers from the base, then patrolling back to the base. While in violation of 7th Air Force and MACV directives, it gave the forces training and experience that proved invaluable during Tet.

Equipment needed to perform their duties was often in short supply or nonexistent. NCOs exercised their initiative to support their forces by working trades for weaponry they otherwise could not obtain. The Security Police supply NCOIC at Tan Son Nhut procured quad-.50 caliber machine guns, considerably more firepower than was available with the standard issue M-60 machine guns, by working with contacts in nearby Army units. These weapons proved highly effective in blunting assaults during Tet.

Perhaps the most cogent statement made regarding the effectiveness of the tactical leadership among the Security Police during Tet was made by Franklin Ybarbo, an Airman during the battle at Tan Son Nhut, who said, "Regardless of how much equipment or training we had, it was enough. The battle was fought and won with nothing but small arms. The American initiative and ingenuity was enough to defeat the enemy." The military during Vietnam was overwhelmingly a conscript force, unlike today's all-volunteer force, but the leadership exhibited during Tet by the Security Police assigned to Tan Son Nhut and Bien Hoa is the kind today's forces would recognize immediately as being effective; doing the right thing for personnel so they can do the mission they have been assigned. The North Vietnamese Army forces attacking the air bases were carrying their dress uniforms in their packs and had been issued new AK-47 assault rifles, with the intent that the bases would be rapidly captured and they could march in a victory parade on the flightlines. The courage and leadership at all levels of the men of the 377 and 3 SPS ensured this never happened. The estimate of NVA killed at Tan Son Nhut alone was placed at over 900, as opposed to 4 Security Policemen and 19 US Army soldiers killed. Tet was an overwhelming loss to the North Vietnamese, thanks in good measure to the men of the Security Police.

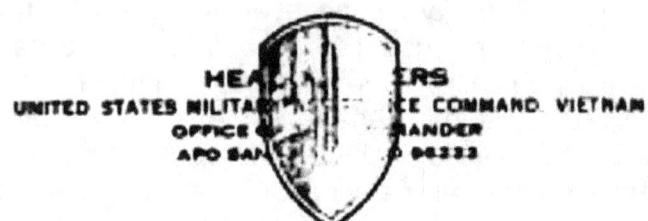

MACJ13   1 6 MAR 1968

SUBJECT: Commendation

TO: Commander
           Seventh Air Force
           APO 96307

    1. The recent Communist Tet Offensive posed a significant challenge to the responsiveness and effectiveness of all our forces in Vietnam. The men of the 377th Security Police Squadron accepted this challenge and helped to frustrate the enemy's intentions. Their defense of Tan Son Nhut Air Base and eventual defeat of the attacking enemy force has reflected the highest traditions of the Air Force. The men of this unit can take pride in the contributions they have made to the allied efforts in Southeast Asia.

    2. Please convey my congratulations to the men of the 377th Security Police Squadron for a job well done.

W. C. WESTMORELAND
General, United States Army
Commanding

LEADERSHIP STUDY FOR OPERATIONAL COMPETENCE:

GENERAL CREECH AND THE TRANSFORMATION OF TACTICAL AIR COMMAND (TAC)

    General Wilbur L. "Bill" Creech was the commander of TAC from 1978 to 1984. Recognizing the multiple demands associated with surviving and performing effectively in the low-altitude arena, General Creech sought an appropriate blend of technology and tactics that might help pilots return to higher altitudes where they could escape the dangers of the low-altitude regime and improve their chances of successful target attack. During earlier Red Flags, all starting scenarios each day presumed that it was the first minute of the first hour of a war against undegraded Warsaw Pact air defenses. No kill removal was provided to account for surface-to-air missiles (SAMs) destroyed in previous missions, and low-level penetration to target was invariably the standard practice, on the premise that radar-guided SAMs could not be negated from higher altitudes. Not only did the resulting simulated loss rate to enemy antiaircraft artillery (AAA) and short-range infrared SAMs soar to a point where many pilots concluded that they could not survive in actual combat, the actual aircraft accident rate rose dramatically as a consequence of the unforgiving nature of the training environment. During the first two years of Red Flag, more than 30 heavily task-saturated aircrews lost their lives as a result of either having flown into the ground inadvertently while maneuvering to avoid getting locked up by a simulated threat radar or having collided in midair during a maneuvering engagement with the aggressors.

This sobering situation starkly underscored what General Creech came to call "go-low disease," motivated by his concern that the emphasis on low-altitude ingress was not only causing a needlessly high accident rate in peacetime training, but also was jeopardizing aircrew survivability and future flexibility in actual combat while, at the same time, constraining TAC's appreciation of the equipment needed to perform the ground-attack mission more effectively. In response, General Creech insisted on new tactics aimed at making defense rollback the first order of business. The emphasis instead swung to developing equipment and tactics that would enable the opening of a medium-altitude window because the most lethal Soviet SAMs could not be successfully underflown within the heart of their engagement envelopes. Aircrew proficiency at low-level operations was maintained as a fallback measure. The new focus concentrated on sanitizing the air defense environment by taking out or neutralizing enemy SAMs as a first priority, so that attacking aircraft could operate more safely as soon as possible at higher altitudes beyond the lethal reach of AAA.

At the same time, General Creech eliminated the initial "core squadron" mission planning practice and instead put TAC's air division commanders in charge of scenarios on a rotating basis. There emerged a heightened emphasis on acquiring the needed equipment that would render medium altitude tactics both possible in principle and also effective. In addition, new capabilities and tactics for operating at night were pushed hard and ultimately validated at Red Flag. Thanks to that, the character of Red Flag shifted notably toward something more closely approximating realistic large-force employment against an enemy whose defenses would eventually be degraded in actual combat. The result was more real-world training realism, as opposed to the false realism of an impenetrable enemy defense, which was finally understood in hindsight to have produced more negative than positive training.

Getting Serious About Electronic Warfare

Closely connected to this stress on greater realism and greater emphasis on enemy air defense suppression was a mounting concern over the need to introduce the complexities of electronic combat into peacetime tactical training, especially those connected with coping effectively in a heavy communications jamming environment. Both during his previous assignment as the commander of the USAF's Electronic Systems Division and later as TAC commander, General Creech figured prominently in this effort to integrate a serious program of offensive and defensive electronic combat into the Air Force's training repertoire. In 1981, he initiated Green Flag, a Red Flag-like exercise conducted biennially at Nellis with special emphasis on electronic warfare and SAM suppression.

During the first Green Flag, General Creech directed that communications jamming be turned on at the outset and left on throughout the operation just as the Soviets would do in actual combat. As a result, 72 percent of the training sorties flown were ineffective. That ended once and for all the assumption that one could overcome enemy jamming efforts merely by manually changing radio frequencies.

TAC Turnaround

Along with the major advances in aircrew training and proficiency outlined above, a largely unsung but nonetheless groundbreaking parallel improvement also took place in the organizational efficiency of TAC during the late 1970s and early 1980s under General Creech's command. Earlier in the 1970s, upward of half of TAC's $25 billion inventory of aircraft were not mission-ready at any given time, and as many as 200 of its 3,800 aircraft were classified as "hangar queens"—grounded for three weeks or more due to a lack of maintenance or needed parts. Moreover, pilots who required a minimum of 20 hours of flying time a month to remain operationally ready were getting only half that amount in most cases.

TAC suffered high maintenance inefficiencies and an unacceptably high accident rate that was partly caused by them. Air Force leadership accommodated this financial crunch by raiding its operations and maintenance accounts. All of this was heavily driven by the top-down management style that had come to afflict the entire US defense establishment as a result of Defense Secretary Robert McNamara's dogma of centralization from the business world which, by the end of the Vietnam war, had pervaded almost all walks of American military life.

Among the many pernicious results of this affliction was a mounting lapse in integrity at the operational level, in which small lies about unit performance became ever larger sins of self-deception which ultimately undermined both mission readiness and safety. Driven by a perceived need to worship statistics for their own sake rather than the underlying facts they were supposed to represent and by a bureaucracy which insisted on hearing the "right" answers irrespective of reality, USAF aircrews would falsify their mission reports to show that they had performed events such as inflight refuelings and weapons deliveries which they had in fact not conducted. Thanks to the same felt compulsion, unit supervisors would record takeoffs which had been delayed by maintenance as "on time" and assign aircraft to the flight schedule which had not been properly released by maintenance control. In sum, bureaucratic gridlock and an overlay of regulations and statistical imperatives, aggravated by diminished funds, had come to stifle morale and to discourage initiative and innovation at the command's grass-roots level.

With the strong backing of Air Force Chief of Staff General David Jones, General Creech quickly sized up the situation and proceeded to invert the traditional top-down centralization of TAC by imposing a strict bottom-up approach to the organization and management of his command, in the process forcing authority and responsibility down to its very lowest reaches. At the same time, he introduced a radically new and different tone by replacing the former pattern of leadership intimidation and bluster with what he called "reasoned command." The new watchword became management through motivation rather than regulation, on the premise that professionals will willingly assume greater responsibility when they are treated with dignity and given a sense of personal ownership of their contribution to the larger whole.

General Creech's leadership philosophy was based on a recognition that loyalty was a two-way street and on the premise that if a commander always looked up to those at the front, he would never talk down to them. It was profoundly intolerant of centrocratic practices and recognized that an organization can only be as successful as those at the bottom are willing to make it. Toward that end, General Creech emphasized focusing more on the product than on the process. He sought to minimize excess regulation, which he believed merely depressed the spirit and stifled motivation. He also sought to replace inhibitions on communication with full openness, and he shifted his headquarters function from restricting to facilitating. Above all, he constantly stressed that there were no poor units, only poor leaders.

General Creech insisted that a mistake was not a crime and a crime was not a mistake, and he incessantly played up the importance of honoring the difference between the two in meting out discipline for mishaps and lesser oversights. His abiding goal was to infuse the system with trust and respect so that coherence and control might be maintained through incentive rather than through top-down authoritarianism. He sought to instill throughout the ranks an appreciation of the crucial difference between quality *control* and quality *creation* and to focus predominantly on the latter, which demanded both different language and a different mindset. To achieve it, he strove to inhibit excess micromanagement of inputs from above. He also spotlighted pride, a quality that needed creating and sustaining by empowering those at the working level to show initiative, while providing for responsibility and accountability at every level.

As General Creech later explained it, "the villain wasn't any particular person, but the whole system." By systematically pushing decisions down to the level of those front-line supervisors who actually carried them out, the risk of poor decisions was sharply reduced. General Creech personally played a lead role in selecting, mentoring, and grooming those at the working level who showed the greatest promise for future leadership, motivated by his credo that the cardinal imperative of a leader is to produce more leaders. His four simple "pass/fail" standards of conduct expected of all subordinate TAC leaders entailed a staunch refusal to countenance any manifestations of lying, displays of temper, abuse of position, or lapses in integrity.

The payoff of this turnaround in the TAC culture soon became widely apparent. Time came to be used more efficiently, quality in all domains of command activity went up, and excellence became a TAC-wide fixation. Units became competitive in all major areas of endeavor, particularly in maintenance delivery and flight operations. Unit commanders were encouraged to fly more often and to lead from the front. All of this generated measurable improvements in all major categories of performance with no more aircraft, personnel, or money than TAC had when General Creech first assumed command. He narrowed the gap in trust between TAC's leaders and led, installed a system based on mutual respect and mutual support, and instilled a quality mindset at every level, basing the product (TAC's organizational efficiency and mission readiness) on persuasion rather than ex cathedra orders. The ensuing effect of reducing the number of TAC's aircraft that were down for maintenance at any given moment by three-fourths yielded an inventory availability and increase in combat capability from existing assets that would have cost more than $12 billion had they been purchased anew.

These reforms eventually permeated all elements of TAC down to the lowest front-line operators, in the process fundamentally changing their former roles, relationships, and responsibilities by enhancing the creativity and commitment of those who ultimately determined the command's success. The impact of the reforms on TAC's morale quotient was palpable. TAC's first-term reenlistment rate increased by 136 percent, a resounding vote of approval for the new, decentralized, and team-based approach to management. Other early returns included a substantial increase in available flying hours for aircrews, better quality of aircraft maintenance, and a sharp increase in TAC's overall mission readiness rates.

Impact of "Robusting"

In a significant departure from previous resource management practice which he called unit "robusting," General Creech dramatically increased the combat capability of TAC's wings simply by applying a new organizing principle. Instead of sharing shortages across all three squadrons in a given wing, as had been the previous practice, General Creech took the existing assets of a wing (both assigned aircrews and aircraft) and built up two of the three squadrons to full strength rather than spreading the pain equally among all three.

The corrective measures instituted by General Creech in 1978, with full Air Staff support, established explicit criteria for "robust" units, namely, those that were manned and equipped at a level that made them ready to meet their wartime tasking. The advantages of this new approach included greater honesty in unit status reporting by highlighting rather than hiding shortages and by sharing a wing's strengths rather than its weaknesses. Robusting made TAC's wings better organized for prompt deployment to meet wartime obligations by preventing the suboptimization of key assets and by putting pressure where it belonged, namely, on resource suppliers so that unit tasking would be more in line with actually available resources.

In all, these reforms lent a sharper focus to authority and accountability and got unit-level peer pressure working in positive rather than negative directions. They also drove authority, accountability, and a sense of ownership to the lowest possible levels throughout TAC, giving everyone in the system both pride of involvement and a personal stake in the product. In short order, TAC went from a vertically- to a horizontally-organized command. Each squadron became responsible for its own 24 assigned aircraft, with all disciplines working together in small teams within the squadron to get the job done. Along the way, paperwork was reduced by 65 percent, and the average time required to deliver a needed part was lowered from three and a half hours to eight minutes. The net result was a genuine personalizing of a once-impersonal system, as well as a doubling of the number of peacetime training sorties flown during a given training period with no increase in operating cost.

In an enduring legacy of the TAC turnaround, this transformation in management style and organizational efficiency instituted during General Creech's tenure later swept the rest of the Air Force. The team-based, decentralized approach to management flowed from the premise that desired accomplishments are achieved by individuals and small collectives working as teams.

LEADERSHIP STUDY FOR STRATEGIC VISION:

SENIOR NONCOMMISSIONED OFFICER LEADERSHIP AND ESTABLISHING A STRATEGIC VISION FOR THE ENLISTED FORCE[56]

> *Every Airman is important to the mission, whatever that mission is. There is no one AFSC or person that is more important than another.*
>
> **—Chief Master Sergeant of the Air Force James A. Roy,**
> **March 2010**

The Air Force enlisted corps comprises over 80% of uniformed Airmen (Active duty, Air National Guard, and Air Force Reserve). Within the enlisted force structure, Air Force senior noncommissioned officers (SNCOs) lead an enlisted corps that is professional, technically competent, and highly motivated. The primary role of the Air Force SNCO is to ensure mission accomplishment by providing highly effective leadership. SNCOs are also responsible for evaluating, developing, and executing the Service's institutional competencies through the NCO corps at all levels of leadership. A critical function of the SNCO is to develop an enlisted force with the required skills and abilities to meet today's peacetime, conflict, and contingency requirements. They emphasize developing leaders with tactical expertise early in their careers, and with operational competence and strategic vision when they reach the SNCO ranks and responsibilities.

Strategic Vision Level

The strategic vision level of the enlisted corps involves senior enlisted leaders (SELs) who have responsibilities for large organizations, and who deal with issues requiring inter-organizational cooperation and extended timelines. Although this

---

[56] Information is a consolidation of interviews conducted in May-June 2010 by Mr David Scott Johnson, Air Force Research Institute, with 15 Chief Master Sergeants (CMSgts), including the Chief Master Sergeant of the Air Force (CMSAF). Each CMSgt was either a Combatant Command, Major Command, numbered Air Force or wing-level Command Chief Master Sergeant or enlisted career field managers at the Air Staff.

strategic level of leadership normally applies to Chief Master Sergeants (CMSgts), it can sometimes include Senior Master Sergeants in higher headquarters positions (Department of Defense, combatant commands, HAF, MAJCOM, direct reporting units, field operating agencies, and select agencies and headquarters).

From the SNCO perspective, strategic vision centers on the development of enlisted Airmen. Taking an enterprise and holistic approach, it sets the deliberate development path for the enlisted force. The SNCO translates this effort into an effective enlisted force development plan by shaping, and navigating in, the environment. It is a broad and encompassing concept that is forward looking and focused on the sustainment, re-evaluation, and development of required competencies necessary to achieve the desired effects in support of the joint force commander. Therefore, the strategic vision as espoused by SELs should outline the expectations for all enlisted Airmen, providing them with a logical, consistent, forward-looking perspective that supports the development of the future SELs in the Air Force.

> *The strategic vision sets the path for everything that we do. It is far-reaching…10-15 years from now. It sets our path; it helps us define what those objectives are, and how we're going to get there.*
>
> **—Chief Master Sergeant of the Air Force James A. Roy, March 2010**

Today's and tomorrow's enlisted Airmen are truly "Strategic Airmen." Our enlisted corps is consistently required to operate outside of the traditional construct of the Air Force in concert with or in support of sister Service, allied, coalition, federal, state, and non-governmental operations. This ability to excel and contribute to our national objectives is achieved by determining the required enlisted force structure necessary to be successfully prepared for future challenges and demands. Once the required force is determined, the SNCO sets the direction, steps, and timeline to reach that end-state. Senior NCOs are leaders.

The Senior Enlisted Leader

> *When explaining to partner nations building an NCO Corps, telling a senior officer their Sergeants Major or Chief doesn't want to be them and is an honest broker on issues, they tend to see the light.*
>
> **—Chief Master Sergeant Chris Muncy Air National Guard Command Chief Master Sergeant, March 2010**

The senior enlisted leader understands what it means to be an Airman from a doctrinal, whole of government, and joint perspective. SELs work closely with senior officers, consistently taking an enterprise-wide whole of government approach, which embraces all levels, and understand commander's intent, their unit's mission, vision, and goals. Not only must SELs understand senior officers' intentions, they must also be able to clearly interpret and articulate that commander's intent to the lowest enlisted levels. They accomplish this by understanding and articulating the linkages that each enlisted member, regardless of rank, has to the overall success of the unit's mission.

The SEL understands and appreciates the future requirements of the enlisted Airmen in the joint, coalition, and interagency environments. In doing so, the SEL is able to complement their senior officer's leadership as they pursue their strategic vision. One of the primary responsibilities of the SEL is to champion the continued professional development of the enlisted corps and take up the mantle of leadership to set future enlisted leaders up for success. SELs are the key stakeholder in maintaining the traditions of the enlisted corps, ensuring these traditions are carried on by future generations of NCOs and SELs.

SELs are strategic advisors and provide the enlisted perspective into the overall strategic vision. They are an integral part of the overall strategic-level decision making process, and are expected to serve as an "honest broker" to the senior leader as well as champion and protect the strategic vision.

The Chief Master Sergeant of the Air Force, Command Chief Master Sergeants, Career Field Managers, and other strategic Chief Master Sergeants

> *My top leadership priority is to create a leadership-centered culture that contributes to a foundation of trust and mutual respect, which drives greater mission success.*
>
> **—Chief Master Sergeant Thomas S. Narofsky,**
> **US Strategic Command Command Chief Master Sergeant**
> **September 2008**

The Chief Master Sergeant of the Air Force, Command Chief Master Sergeants, and enlisted career field managers have diverse backgrounds with experience at the squadron, wing, headquarters, joint, and combatant command levels. Having an enterprise-wide perspective, they are politically savvy and have developed relationships with the other Service senior enlisted leaders. These SELs also follow a deliberate developmental path, building on people/team and organizational competencies, which leads to the creation of effective institutional leadership competencies. Overall, the Chief Master Sergeant of the Air Force will have a balanced and diverse career built on a foundation of deliberate tactical, operational, and strategic leadership education and training, varying assignments at all levels within the Air Force, and joint experience.

Enlisted Development

The Air Force needs a long-term, focused organizational strategy of investing in our Airmen by leveraging our skills, talents, and experiences to transform our Airman into future strategic enlisted leaders.

**—Chief Master Sergeant Thomas S. Narofsky,
US Strategic Command Command Chief Master Sergeant
September 2008**

The enlisted role is not centered around the individual, it is about service; service to the Nation, the Air Force, and to the unit. As a result, the Air force takes a deliberate approach to enlisted force development, which includes career progression with increased levels of supervisory, leadership, and managerial responsibilities. The foundation of the enlisted force development is the institutional competencies that provide the common force developmental language and represent the leadership, management, and warrior ethos qualities required of all Airmen.

Professional military education (PME) plays a key role in the overall development of enlisted Airmen. PME is part of the enlisted continuum of education, which begins when they enter the Air Force and continues throughout their careers. Although the Air Force provides a wide range of educational schools, courses, programs and opportunities, each enlisted member also has a personal responsibility for his or her own professional and personal development. Because education is essential for the development of enlisted Airmen, they are not only expected but highly encouraged to actively pursue educational and experiential opportunities throughout their careers. Airmen should also be educated in their roles associated with the Air Force's interagency partners. Off-duty education provides development by enhancing one's intellectual capability, capacity, and critical thinking skills. Moreover, diverse personal and professional developmental paths provide our Airmen opportunities to undertake varying degrees of challenges and build problem solving skills derived from new knowledge and experiences.

Support of Enduring Deployments and Contingency Operations

Enduring deployments and continued support of contingency operations have resulted in the most combat-hardened force that we have ever had in the Air Force.

**—Chief Master Sergeant of the Air Force James A. Roy,
March 2010**

Support of enduring deployments and contingency operations creates a better, more culturally aware enlisted corps. Due to the wide range of mission sets and support requirements, such as joint expeditionary tasking and coalition support assignments, our combat hardened enlisted corps often performs duties outside of its specifically-trained specialty. The result is a more well-rounded and experienced enlisted member with joint, coalition, and whole-of-government perspectives. As a result, the enlisted corps is capable of taking on new roles and missions in support of the ever-changing global environment. In the past, enlisted Airmen were only assigned duties within their specialty fields. It was uncommon to find enlisted members working outside of their specific specialty code. Today, the Air Force enlisted member can be found across the battlespace supporting the joint force commander in many different ways. The professional enlisted corps has transitioned from an attitude of "it's not my job," when asked to perform non-specialty code tasks to "what can I do to help make the mission a success," regardless of what Service or nation they are supporting.

Enlisted Joint Perspectives

> *Having a Joint perspective is extremely important. Today, we don't do anything by ourselves. We do it as a joint/coalition team. We gain our strength through diversity.*
>
> **—Chief Master Sergeant of the Air Force James A. Roy,**
> **March 2010**

Today's Airmen, across the entire Air Force, develop a joint perspective early in their careers. For some career fields that have similar technical foundations, such as medical and explosive ordnance disposal, initial training is conducted in a joint environment. This joint perspective provides an understanding of other Service cultures, competencies, and terminologies, while preserving the Air Force culture. The enlisted force should understand the core competencies that Soldiers, Sailors, and Marines are educated and trained in and employ. This provides them a much greater understanding of their responsibilities to execute operations with a strategic vision, but also understand how their Air Force competencies merge with our sister Services. Understanding of culture, responsibilities and shared competencies builds early interoperability that is necessary for immediate success in the joint/deployed environment.

Airmen should also be educated in their roles associated with the Air Force's interagency partners. Enlisted Airmen work daily to support U.S. Northern Command as they defend the homeland. Through the National Incident Management System (NIMS) military members are always subordinate to an interagency or local responder. They don't take over; they enhance capabilities to save lives, property and secure the homeland.

All Airmen should have a thorough understanding of the contributions of all joint and total force Services. In-depth perspectives and the ability to think multi-dimensionally are becoming increasingly important as the global nature of Air Force operations demand that Airmen continue to deploy jointly.

Future Role of the Enlisted Airman

Throughout the history of the Air Force, enlisted Airmen have often performed the same functions as officers. For example, during the early days of the Air Force, the first pilots and instructor pilots were enlisted. Since then, certain officer-only career fields have successfully transitioned to the enlisted force. An example of this is in space and cyberspace operations, where a growing number of enlisted Airmen are becoming key to those operations. Undoubtedly, the future will see even more traditional officer-only duties being introduced to the enlisted corps. These emerging career fields will be manned by highly skilled, trained, computer/technology savvy, and adaptable enlisted Airmen.

As the Air Force continues to reexamine technical skill set requirements in the application of airpower across the full spectrum of operations, especially with emerging technologies, enlisted Airmen will have greater opportunities to expand their specialty areas as critical team members. This will allow officers to better function in leadership positions that develop and lead strategic vision while the enlisted Airmen carry out those visions.

GLOSSARY

Abbreviations and Acronyms

AAA	antiaircraft artillery
AFDD	Air Force doctrine document
AFI	Air Force instruction
AFM	Air Force manual
AFPAM	Air Force pamphlet
AFPD	Air Force policy directive
AFSC	Air Force specialty code
ARVN	Army of the Republic of Vietnam
CMSAF	Chief Master Sergeant of the Air Force
CoL	continuum of learning
CSAF	Chief of Staff, United States Air Force
CSC	central security control
DAF	Department of the Air Force
DOD	Department of Defense
HAF	Headquarters, Air Force
IC	institutional competency
JDOC	joint defense operations center
MACV	Military Assistance Command-Vietnam
MAJCOM	major command
MLR	main line of resistance
NCO	noncommissioned officer
NIMS	National Incident Management System
NVA	North Vietnamese Army
PME	professional military education
POL	petroleum, oil, lubricants
QRF	quick reaction force
QRT	quick reaction team
RPG	rocket-propelled grenade
SAM	surface-to-air missile
SAT	security alert team
SECAF	Secretary of the Air Force

SEL	senior enlisted leaders
SNCO	senior noncommissioned officer
SPS	security police squadron
TAC	Tactical Air Command
TF	task force
U.S.C.	United States Code
VC	Viet Cong

Definitions

continuum of learning. A career-long process of individual development where challenging experiences are combined with education and training through a common taxonomy to produce Airmen who possess the tactical expertise, operational competence, and strategic vision to lead and execute the full spectrum of Air Force missions. (AFDD 1-1)

core values. A statement of those institutional values and principles of conduct that provide the moral framework within which military activities take place. The professional Air Force ethic consists of three fundamental and enduring values of integrity, service before self, and excellence in all we do. (AFDD 1-1)

doctrine. Fundamental principles by which the military forces or elements thereof guide their actions in support of national objectives. It is authoritative but requires judgment in application. (JP 1–02)

force development. A deliberate process of preparing Airmen through the continuum of learning with the required competencies to meet the challenges of current and future operating environments. (AFDD 1-1)

institutional competencies. A measurable cluster of skills, knowledge, and abilities required of all Airmen and needed to operate successfully in a constantly changing environment. (AFDD 1-1)

leadership. The art and science of motivating, influencing, and directing Airmen to understand and accomplish the Air Force mission. (AFDD 1-1)

www.ingramcontent.com/pod-product-compliance
Lightning Source LLC
Chambersburg PA
CBHW080316290526
45790CB00005B/2067